you know you're in
georgia when ...

Some Other Books in the Series

You Know You're in Arizona When . . .

You Know You're in California When . . .

You Know You're in Florida When . . .

You Know You're in Illinois When . . .

You Know You're in Kansas When . . .

You Know You're in Massachusetts When . . .

You Know You're in Michigan When . . .

You Know You're in Minnesota When . . .

You Know You're in New Hampshire When . . .

You Know You're in New Jersey When . . .

You Know You're in Rhode Island When . . .

You Know You're in Texas When . . .

You Know You're in Washington When . . .

You Know You're In Series

you know you're in
georgia when …

**101 Quintessential Places, People, Events,
Customs, Lingo, and Eats of the Peach State**

William Schemmel

INSIDERS' GUIDE®

GUILFORD, CONNECTICUT
AN IMPRINT OF THE GLOBE PEQUOT PRESS

INSIDERS' GUIDE®

Illustrations by Sue Mattero

Library of Congress Cataloging-in-Publication Data is available.

ISBN 978-0-7627-4131-1

Manufactured in the United States of America
First Edition/First Printing

To Roscoe, my good and faithful friend.

about the author

William Schemmel has spent almost his whole lifetime "knowing" about Georgia. Globe Pequot recently published the eighth edition of his *Georgia Off the Beaten Path,* and this year will publish *Georgia Curiosities,* second edition. Based in Decatur, Georgia, he writes frequently about the state and other exotic destinations for major newspapers and magazines.

to the reader

I've known Georgia since FDR was president. In the ensuing six decades, the state has changed monumentally. Nowadays, we're the ninth most populous state, with 9 million residents and counting way too rapidly. If you're among the millions of newcomers, there are certain fundamental truths still self-evident: Grits is groceries. The Gnat Line is crossed with great caution and ample supplies of repellent. There's a Waffle House, or two, on every corner, and Chick-Fil-A is never on Sunday. If you stand still too long in mid-summer, the kudzu will get you, even if the gnats and no-see-'ems don't. Georgia isn't Oregon or Maine—when summer arrives in early June, it sticks around, hot and sticky, into way late in September. Before Global Warming, Atlanta and other northerly sections were usually blanketed with a few inches of snow every winter, and ice storms knocked the flimsy pine trees over on the power lines and those whose homes had fireplaces discovered they had a lot of grateful neighbors. Nowadays, the only snow falls in the really high places in the mountains. As you'll discover, it's a beautiful state, with mostly-friendly people and a lot of quirky places you'll get to know as you venture across them. I hope you enjoy using this book as your guide.

Talk about user-friendly. Georgia's highest waterfall, 729-foot Amicalola Falls, near Dawsonville in northeast Georgia, is clearly visible from the state park's parking lot. Visitors can sit in their vehicles, or walk just a few steps, to take in the beauty of one of the state's most scenic natural wonders. At the base of the falls, a placid pool is a convenient place for anglers to try their luck.

Amicalola (Amee-caw-lo-la) is a Cherokee word that means "tumbling waters." To get a sense of how steep the tumbling cascade of eastern America's most precipitous waterfall really is, hike or drive up the sharply graded road to the top of the falls. A short walk along a planked path leads to the falls' overlook. Don't lean over too far, or you, too, may take a tumble.

For those up for more strenuous exercise, there are several options. Five miles of trails wind around the falls and through the woods and mountains. Even if you're not intent on hiking the Appalachian Trail's 2,250 miles to Maine, you can get a taste of it on the 8-mile approach trail to Springer Mountain, the trail's southern terminus. Cabins and guest rooms in the Amicalola Falls Lodge are the last comfort that hikers experience before hitting the trail.

Amicalola is also the start of a 5-miler to the Len Foote Hike Inn, a rustic hideaway with bunk beds and family-style chow. Also

Amicalola Falls:

Native Americans called the northeast Georgia cataract "tumbling waters."

in the state park are tent, trailer, and RV sites as well as picnic shelters, playgrounds, trout streams, interpretive programs, and a ropes course. Kangaroos are hopping a few miles away, and there's gold in them thar hills.

Springer Mountain in northeast Georgia is the Alpha and the Omega of the Appalachian Trail (AT). Depending on which way you're hiking, it's either your entree or egress on the 2,500-mile journey from Georgia to Mount Katahdin, Maine. From Springer the trail winds 79 miles across the state, passing through woods and over 4,500-foot mountains.

At Neels Gap the trail crosses Highway 19/129 and goes "indoors" as it passes through a covered breezeway of the Mountain Crossing/Walasi-Y1 Center, a stone-and-log legacy of the Depression—era Civilian Conservation Corps. Trail information, supplies and camping gear, sandwiches, hot showers, ice cream, and sympathy are available there. The proprietors do their best to persuade wafflers to stay the course a little longer and otherwise will arrange transportation back to the airport in Atlanta.

If hikers go on, Section III is a moderately difficult 5.7 miles to Tesnatee Gap on the Richard Russell Scenic Byway (Highway 348), where tenderfeet can step on for a mile or a few yards. At Bly Gap the trail bids Georgia adieu and crosses into North Carolina's Great Smoky Mountains National Park.

A Walk in the Woods, Bill Bryson's often-serious, very humorous 1996 nonfiction account of his trek on the AT with out-of-shape comrade Steven Katz, is a must-read for any aspiring adventurer.

Just getting to Springer Mountain almost kayoed the hikers' walk before it started. As Bryson and Katz labored up the 7-mile approach trail on an 11-degree March morning, their backs and legs groaned under the weight of overloaded packs. They jettisoned peanut butter, Snickers bars, Spam, rice, and brown sugar but nearly called it quits at breakfast their first day. "I can't believe you left the Little Debbies," Katz said, and immediately began to fall behind.

Appalachian Trail:

Mount Katahdin, here we come! The journey of 2,500 miles begins at Springer Mountain in northeast Georgia.

...following the Atlanta Braves is like blasting off on *Apollo 13,* every blasted year

In April 1970 the three-man crew of *Apollo 13* rocketed off from Cape Canaveral with the goal of being the third NASA mission to land on the moon. It was not to be. Before they got there an oxygen tank exploded, and astronaut John (Jack) Swigert coined the understatement, "Okay, Houston, we've had a problem here."

On their wing-and-a-lot-of-prayers return to Earth, the crew passed within about 400 tantalizing miles of the moon's surface. They made it back safely, but neither Swigert nor his crewmates Fred Haise and James Lovell ever had a chance to moonwalk.

During the 1990s and the early years of the first decade of the 21st century, the Atlanta Braves also had "a problem" getting to their personal moon, a World Series championship. From 1991 through 2005, the Braves won 14 National League division championships and 5 league championships. Each year, as the playoffs approached, Braves fans held their breath, crossed their fingers, burned candles, and said prayers that this would be the year. But only in 1995, when the Braves defeated the American League champion Cleveland Indians, did they come through as World Champions.

So one of the winningest teams in professional sports has become the Big Peach's greatest heartache. Which makes many a fan wonder: Would it have been better not to have won at all? Naw.

Atlanta Braves:

Maybe "next year" they'll win another World Series.

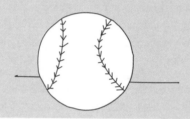

After moving from Boston—where at various times they were called the Red Caps, Doves, Rustlers, Bees, and Beaneaters—and then from Milwaukee in 1965, the Braves won two division titles: in 1969 and 1983. Then they went into the Dark Ages, where winning seasons were as rare as Georgia peaches in January. Before they started their remarkable "worst to first" transformation, the Braves ended the 1990 season with 65 wins and 97 losses. In 1991 they won 94 and lost 68, then the league championship was theirs when Sid Bream slid into home with the winning run against the Pittsburgh Pirates.

During the prolonged drought Hank Aaron was one of the few bright lights, breaking Babe Ruth's nearly 50-year-old home-run record on April 8, 1974. That day Aaron clouted his 715th round-tripper in Atlanta-Fulton County Stadium.

3

you know you're in
georgia when ...
... you're in the once-Olympic city

Atlanta's Olympic summer was more than a decade ago, but souvenirs of its two weeks in the international sun are all around town. Sitting at Turner Field, watching the Braves, you're actually in the Olympic Stadium, where opening and closing ceremonies bookended the feats of runners, jumpers, pole vaulters, and hurlers of unwieldy things.

When the Games were done, the Braves knocked out 30,000 seats and added a food court, restaurants, bars, a museum, a kids' play area, sky boxes, and other diversions. The Olympic Torch, where Muhammad Ali climbed the stairs and lit the caldron flame to dramatically open the Games, was moved down the street. Even ardent civic boosters reluctantly agree with critics, who lampooned it as the world's largest McDonald's french-fry carton.

Centennial Olympic Park, impresario Billy Payne's vision of a town square where participants and fans could gather between events, is the most spectacular legacy. Created from 22 acres of vacant lots and broken-down buildings, the park is the engine sparking ongoing downtown revival. Children and adults picnic on the lawns and splash in the choreographed Five Rings Fountain. Payne's bronze likeness looks benignly on concerts, festivals, July 4 fireworks, and other events. The Olympic Vil-

Atlanta Olympics:

Atlanta still cherishes its 15 minutes in the international limelight.

lage apartments now house Georgia State University scholars.

The Centennial Olympics Games Museum, located on the grounds of the Atlanta History Center north of downtown, captures the entire Olympic experience. Films, photos, memorabilia, and interactive exhibits trace Atlanta's Olympic saga back to 1987, when Payne and a small group of friends first suggested that an improbable dream really was possible. Even Izzy, the much-abused Games mascot, has his day.

4

Berry College in Rome, Georgia, sits on the world's largest educational campus—more than 28,000 acres. The school began in the early 1900s, when Miss Martha Berry became concerned about the lack of educational opportunities for poor Appalachian Mountain youngsters. In 1902 she used 83 acres inherited from her wealthy father to found the Boys Industrial School; later she added a girls' school and junior college.

The junior college grew into a four-year liberal arts college that graduated its first class in 1934; graduate classes were added in 1972.

Berry required her students to work for part of their tuition. She believed that diligent labor promoted students' sense of responsibility and self-worth. The work program also helped the college keep operating expenses low.

After gaining accreditation from the Southern Association of Colleges and Secondary Schools in 1957, the college did away with the work-study program to place greater emphasis on academic programs. However, a large percentage of Berry's 2,100 students still work to offset their fees and earn money for other expenses.

Berry's idealistic approach to education—and her relentless fund-raising—attracted the attention of some of the country's leading philanthropists, including auto magnate Henry Ford, who funded the English Gothic–style Ford Complex in 1924. Berry used some of the donations to purchase 28,000 acres of increasingly valuable land. In recent years education magazines and organizations have named Berry College one of the Southeast's best liberal arts colleges.

Berry died in 1942. The history of her school (sometimes called the "miracle in the mountains") is documented through exhibits, photos, and film in the Martha Berry Museum. Students also lead visitors through Oak Hill, Berry's Greek Revival home.

Berry College:

This "miracle in the mountains" sits on more than 28,000 acres, making it the world's largest educational campus.

you know you're in
georgia when...
...the big one didn't get away

On a June morning in 1932, George Perry, a 20-year-old Telfair County farmer, went fishing and came home with a whopper.

Perry and a fishing buddy had driven down muddy rural roads to Montgomery Lake, a small, shallow arm of the Ocmulgee River. They paddled a homemade boat between swampy sweet gum and cypress roots, and Perry began casting with only two lures in his tackle box. After a few minutes he felt a strong pull on his line and feared that his precious lure had snagged on an underwater stump. It wasn't a stump. It was a world-champion bass.

The 22-pound, 4-ounce largemouth bass was the world-record catch, a true-to-life, no-fish-story tale that put the soft-spoken Perry in the International Game Fish Association's record book and made him a local folk hero. For 74 years he was the Babe Ruth and Hank Aaron of game fishing. He rarely spoke of the record, which he took to the grave with him when he died in 1974.

Perry's big fish went unchallenged until 2006, when three Californians claimed a 25-pound, 1-ounce bass. The bass-fishing community was immediately skeptical. It soon came out that the Californians' fish had been hooked in the side—or "foul-hooked," in the sport's terminology. The International Game Fish Association doesn't recognize foul hooks.

The fish had been weighed on a hand scale, another IGFA no-no. No measurements had been taken, either, and after the fishermen were photographed with their catch, they had released it. All of this refuted the men's claim. In the spirit of good sportsmanship, they declared, "We want to be 100 percent, with no controversy. We plan to be back with a world-record bass that can't be questioned."

Until they do, Perry still wears the crown, and Telfair County has the record and historic markers to prove it.

Big Bass:

George Perry's catch has been the world record-holder since 1932.

Barbecue is the quintessential Georgia cuisine. Scholars debate the "true" 'cue. Fistfights break out over who prepares the paragon of ribs and pulled pork. Georgia barbecue is tomato-based, and beyond that it's up to the individual barbecuemeister's creativity.

In Vienna, in Dooly County, where most Viennese wouldn't know a Sacher torte from a strawberry shortcake, the issue is more or less settled the second weekend of October. That's when the Austrian capital's southeast Georgia namesake (pronounced "VIE-en-na") stages the Big Pig Jig, the state's annual barbecuing championship. Winners go to Memphis in May, to the barbecue art's World Series and Super Bowl, and the great debate simmers down 'til the next year.

The event that now attracts dozens of cooking teams and more than 35,000 spectators began as a simple wager back in 1982. Tired of debating who prepared the most stellar 'cue, the masters of the art decided to put on a barbecue-cooking competition, linked with the county livestock association's annual hog show.

Neutral judges from as far away as Atlanta and Cordele sampled the entries from 20 cooking teams and awarded modest prize money and blue ribbons. A few hundred spectators tipsy on the aromas drifted over to the festival grounds on Interstate 75. It

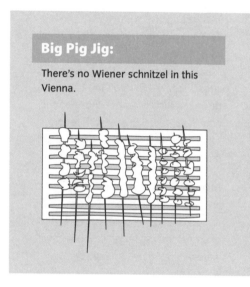

Big Pig Jig:

There's no Wiener schnitzel in this Vienna.

was such a success that people wanted to do it again the following year. So they have, ever since.

From small beginnings, this little piggy has grown into one of Georgia's premiere fall events. It's a lot of good old-fashioned fun. Cooking teams dress up like "MASH" units, pirates, cartoon and movie characters, football and baseball teams, and other themes.

Look pitiful enough, and they might let you sample their shoulders, ribs, butts (pardon the expression), and bubbling cauldrons of Brunswick stew. But if you ask the contenders what's in their secret sauce, they'll reply, "I could tell ya, but then I'd hafta kill ya."

...you remember the Great Blizzard of 1993

Thanks to global warning, we're not likely ever again to see the likes of the Great Blizzard of 1993 (aka "The Superstorm" and "The Storm of the Century"). One of the largest storms in more than 100 years, the mid-March blizzard blindsided the entire Eastern Seaboard with record-breaking low temperatures, snow, and howling, hurricane-force winds.

Atlanta and other Southern cities—where average mid-March temps are in the 50s and 60s and once- or twice-a-year snowfalls of an inch or less make for a brief holiday— were paralyzed by foot-high snow and Arctic cold.

The Great One began in the mountains of New York and New England early on March 12, picked up in intensity as it moved through the Mid-Atlantic states, and then pummeled Washington, D.C. It buried the North Carolina mountains in 50 to 60 inches of snow and ice before moving into Georgia and setting its sights on Atlanta.

TV weather forecasters who predicted flurries and light accumulations ate bountiful crow when an official 10 inches fell over the metropolis like a giant cold marshmallow from outer space. Panicked shoppers stripped supermarket shelves of milk and bread. The city's hilly streets were like a bumper car ride at the county fair, as drivers with no chains or snow tires

Blizzard of 1993:

Hopefully, we will never see its like again.

hydroplaned and collided on snow and black ice.

Travelers on snowbound Interstate 75 between Atlanta and Chattanooga abandoned their cars and took refuge for nearly a week in motels, churches, and schools and relied upon the kindness of strangers.

Dogwoods and azaleas, seduced into bloom by balmy pre-spring, were cruelly ambushed. Southward the storm went, dusting Macon, Augusta, Valdosta, Savannah's picturesque squares and fountains, and gators in the Okefenokee.

When the storm blew itself out, refugees came out of hiding, swapped war stories, and said, "That was a humdinger, wasn't it?"

Brasstown Bald, in Union and Towns Counties, is as high as you can go in Georgia. At 4,784 feet above mean sea level, it looms over the southern end of the Appalachian chain.

You can drive most of the way up Brasstown on a steep, winding, paved road. Be sure your vehicle is up to the task, as many a city-bred sedan blows its radiator along the way. A four-wheel-drive usually does it with ease.

There is a paved parking area ½ mile from the summit. Lace up your Reeboks and hike the rest of the way on the almost-straight-up Brasstown Bald Trail. Catch your breath on the observation deck, where you can take in 360-degree vistas of northern Georgia, Tennessee, and the Carolinas. Lucky you if the fall foliage is in all its scarlet-and-gold glory.

Exhibits in the summit museum decipher the natural and human history of the mountain's environment. It's called a *bald* because of the treeless meadow at the summit. The Depression–era Civilian Conservation Corps built the observation tower primarily for fire observation. It's off-limits to the public.

In 1540 Hernando de Soto and his Spanish merry men touring the area may have climbed Brasstown, like the proverbial bear, to see what they could see. They were looking for gold, and unbeknownst to them, they were most likely walking right over where it would be discovered 300 years later.

De Soto Falls, near Dahlonega, got its name from an unverified tale about a piece of breastplate armor found near the falls; the armor may have belonged to one of Hernando's companions. They clashed with Native Americans, figuring that the Indians knew where the gold was but wouldn't tell. Finally, with sagging spirits and ungilded pockets, the explorers continued west to Memphis, where all they found was the Mississippi River. They were a few centuries too early to discover Elvis.

Brasstown Bald:

Hernando de Soto slept there. (Maybe.)

you know you're in
georgia when...
...you're on the Rocks

You're deep in the heart of southeast Georgia, but for a few discombobulating moments inside the Broxton Rocks Preserve, you might wonder if you've wandered into a tropical rain forest.

A rocky outcropping in the sandy coastal plain, the 3,799-acre preserve is a beautiful, mysterious place where snakes slither among mosses and orchids and dish-size poison ivy leaves glisten seductively in sunlight seeping though longleaf pines and hardwoods.

The Rocks are part of a 15,000-square-mile band of subsurface sandstone known as the Altamaha Grit. In rainy periods Rocky Creek—a 4-mile tributary of the Ocmulgee River—gushes over rock ledges, creating roaring waterfalls. In dry seasons the creek slows to a trickle.

More than 500 species of plants thrive here. Cavelike recesses in the rocks are a moist, shady environment for the green fly orchid and partridge berry, normally more at home in the north Georgia mountains. The crevices are also ideal for the shoestring fern, a long way from its familiar home in the tropics.

About 100 bird species and a host of mammals and reptiles make their home in the Rocks. The forests are sanctuaries for eastern diamondback rattlesnakes, threatened indigo snakes, and coral snakes. They share the sandy landscape, and sometimes the burrows, of the gopher tortoise, Georgia's state reptile. Turkey vultures and wood rats nest in the Rocks. Other residents include horned owls, screech owls, and flying squirrels.

The Douglas Welcome Center (912–384–4555) offers guided tours in March, April, May, September, and October. Hikers are screened to ensure that they are up to the 1½-mile trek through rugged, slippery terrain, where humidity rivals the Amazon and where ticks, mosquitoes, and chiggers feast on tender skin.

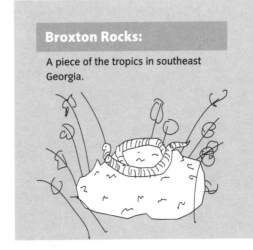

Broxton Rocks:

A piece of the tropics in southeast Georgia.

you know you're in
georgia when...
...you haven't a 'cue without Brunswick stew

Like a hot dog without mustard and relish, or peach cobbler without vanilla ice cream, a plate of Georgia barbecue would be stark naked without its faithful companion, Brunswick stew.

Basically tomato-based, the stew gets its character from lima beans, corn, potatoes, pepper sauce, brown sugar, onions, chicken, pork, and sometimes beef. For real authenticity, some recipes hearken back to the stew's origins and insist on squirrel, rabbit, and/or deer meat. One of the stew's beauties is that you can look at 100 recipes and no two will be exactly alike. And you can make the stew your own with your special touches.

A debate as spicy as the dish itself centers on where Brunswick stew was originally created. A plaque with a cast-iron cooking pot near downtown Brunswick, Georgia, asserts that the very first Brunswick stew was prepared on July 2, 1898, by a cook on St. Simons Island, just off the coast.

Virginians counter that the camp chef for a state politician threw the recipe together with what was at hand during an 1828 hunting expedition in Brunswick County, Virginia.

Brunswick Stew:

Georgia named it, Georgia claims it (although so does Virginia).

The stew is served throughout Georgia and in large areas of Virginia, but it rarely makes an appearance in North Carolina, which has its own vinegar-based sauce and tops its barbecue with coleslaw.

you know you're in
georgia when...
...buzzards are welcomed home to roost

As certain as the swallows returning to California's Mission San Juan Capistrano every spring, buzzards find their way back to Reed Bingham State Park, near Adel (pronounced "a-DELL") the first Saturday of each December.

The homely birds' arrival is heralded by throngs of gawking humans who turn out for "Buzzard Day" nature talks, bird walks, and other festive happenings. Those who can't make the homecoming party can view the "guests" any time until they fly off again in early spring.

Reed Bingham's two types—turkey and black—roost in plain sight in the trees on the swampy banks of the Little River, which flows through the park into a 375-acre lake. As many as 5,000 birds bask in the warm south Georgia sunshine, soar on air currents with wings spread 6 feet wide, and generally have as high an old time as it's possible for their kind to have.

Buzzards:

Keep an eye on Spot and the young'uns at Reed Bingham State Park.

Why do they come to this remote state park? "I don't know, they just do, always have," a park ranger says. What do they eat? "Road kill, mostly." Are children and pets in peril? "Only if they're real small and don't move for a spell."

Time was, Erskine Caldwell was synonymous in Georgians' mind with the general who burned Atlanta and marched off to Savannah. The son of a Presbyterian minister, Caldwell was born in 1903 in the church manse, near Moreland, the town that also gave the literary world Lewis Grizzard. He was a youngster when his father accepted another assignment and moved the family out of Georgia.

As a young man Caldwell went from job to job and saw firsthand the hard life of poor common laborers. In 1932 his first major novel, *Tobacco Road,* about the plight of poor Southern sharecroppers, was critically praised.

Perhaps because the book had the painful sting of undeniable truth, Georgians and other Southerners denounced Caldwell as a pariah. A year later *God's Little Acre*—also about poor rural whites, racism, and the tenant farming system—stirred more controversy.

When the New York Society for the Prevention of Vice tried to prohibit the sale of the novel, Caldwell went to court and, with the testimony of respected critics H. L. Mencken and Sherwood Anderson, won his case. Thanks to the controversy, *God's Little Acre* sold more than 14 million copies. By the late 1940s Caldwell had sold more books than any author in American history.

In 1991 his childhood manse was moved to Moreland's town square and converted into the Erskine Caldwell Birthplace and Museum. About 1,000 visitors a year come to see exhibits on his life, his 50 novels in many languages, and his typewriter, clothing, wedding ring, and other personal effects.

Caldwell, who died in 1987, was one of the first 14 authors inducted in the Georgia Writers Hall of Fame. The University of Georgia Press has republished several of his novels and short stories.

Caldwell, Erskine:

The author traveled from tiny Moreland to *Tobacco Road* and *God's Little Acre.*

Driving U.S. Highway 29, you spy a rusty historical marker on the side of the road 3 miles south of Hartwell and screech to a sudden halt. Skid marks around the marker testify that other motorists have also been taken by surprise by the sign posted by the Georgia Historical Commission in 1954.

The sign reads: "CENTER OF THE WORLD: THIS WAS AH-YEH-LI A-LO-HEE, THE CENTER OF THE WORLD, TO THE CHEROKEE INDIANS. TO THIS ASSEMBLY GROUND, FROM WHICH TRAILS RADIATE IN MANY DIRECTIONS, THEY CAME TO HOLD THEIR COUNCILS, TO DANCE AND WORSHIP, WHICH WERE TO THEM RELATED FUNCTIONS. . . ."

On a small rise near the headwaters of four creeks, at the junction of numerous trails going in all directions, Ah-Yeh-Li was the site of tribal councils and trade—so the designation made sense, at least until people showed up from the other Center of the World (Europe). Some Cherokee still believe the site has mystical powers.

Beside the marker a lopsided chunk of granite, put up by the Benson Chapter of the Daughters of the American Revolution, is a vain effort to atone for the wrongs done to the Cherokee, who were uprooted from the center of their world by President Andrew Jackson. He put them on the Trail of Tears to Oklahoma in the 1830s.

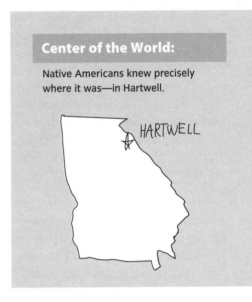

Center of the World:

Native Americans knew precisely where it was—in Hartwell.

HARTWELL

Hartwell was once a popular roosting place for migrating passenger pigeons. Unlike the Cherokee, who have managed to survive, the pigeons couldn't sustain humankind's onslaught and have been extinct since World War I.

In Atlanta they ask first off where you work; in Augusta, who's your family; and in Macon, where you go to church. In Savannah, it's what you want to drink.

The city's founding father, General James Edward Oglethorpe, banned the manufacture, sale, and consumption of rum and other potent beverages. But with the stress of building the capital of a colony named in honor of His Majesty King George II, compounded by the heat, humidity, and infernal bugs, the general's edict was largely winked at.

Members of the Chatham Artillery, founded in 1786 as Georgia's oldest military organization, steeled themselves for cotillions and other battlefronts by quaffing a sweet-tasting but potentially lethal cocktail named in their honor. The drink's origins are unknown, but legend has it that Savannah's genteel ladies mixed the first mild batches and over the years Artillery officers doused it with additional firepower.

On a 1791 visit to Savannah, where he was saluted by 26 firings of the Artillery's heavy guns, General George Washington, who enjoyed his tipples, reputedly got so giddy on the punch that he donated the "Washington Guns," captured from the British at the Battle of Yorktown in 1781. They are still stationed near the riverfront, ready for any Redcoats that might be hiding in the palmetto thickets.

The recipe for Chatham Artillery Punch is a long list of potent ingredients, including gin, wine, Benedictine, rye whiskey, rum, brandy, brown sugar, and unsweetened tea. After the punch steeps for 36 to 48 hours, a case of champagne is added. A brass button from a Confederate officer's uniform is optional. One gobletful will make you happy; two will have you singing Johnny Mercer's "Hooray for Hollywood."

Chatham Artillery Punch:

General Oglethorpe banned this concoction and lawyers, with equal success.

georgia when...

...you're Shootin' the 'Hooch

The Chattahoochee is Georgia's Amazon and Nile, its mini-Mississippi. It comes out of the Blue Ridge Mountains as a clear, cold mountain stream, bursting with youthful energy and a wealth of brown, brook, and rainbow trout begging for the frying pan. In a big hurry to get out of the mountains, the river descends more than 1,500 feet over about 20 miles as it burbles through the town of Helen's faux-Bavarian village.

The name *Chattahoochee* is a Creek Indian word for "painted rocks," a reference to the colorful granite outcroppings along the river's shores. Nineteenth-century Macon poet Sidney Lanier romanticized the waterway in his lyrical "Song of the Chattahoochee":

Out of the hills of Habersham
Down the valleys of Hall,
I hurry amain to reach the plain . . .

Before it can reach that plain some 400 miles southwest of its birthplace, the river fills Lake Sidney Lanier's 520-mile shoreline and runs the gauntlet of metro Atlanta, where it supplies the populace with drinking water and serves as the flowing stage of a summer ritual called Shootin' the 'Hooch.

On sizzling June, July, and August afternoons, thousands beat the heat by bobbing on rafts, tubes, and kayaks over the 'Hooch's gentle Class I and Class II rapids. A companion raft, with a cooler of refreshments and a pet or two, is a traditional part of the experience of making one's way downstream through a portion of the 48-mile Chattahoochee River National Recreation Area. "Painted rocks" along the banks are launching pads for cannonballers.

When rafters and tubers come out—windblown, sunburned, mud-smeared, and under the influence of refreshments—they can say they've got a true Atlanta experience tucked in their cutoffs.

Free of the city, the 'Hooch bends southwestward, forms the Georgia/Alabama border, joins the Flint at Lake Seminole, and flows across the Florida Panhandle as the Apalachicola, into the Gulf of Mexico. Far from the hills of Habersham, far from the 'Hooch shooters in Hotlanna.

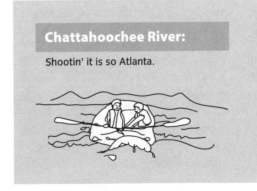

Chattahoochee River:

Shootin' it is so Atlanta.

you know you're in
georgia when...
...you're in America's cherry blossom capital

So what if Macon doesn't have a Tidal Basin and monuments to Jefferson and Lincoln? It's got the Ocmulgee River, Ocmulgee Mounds, Otis Redding, Little Richard, Hay House, Old Cannonball House, the Georgia Music Hall of Fame, the Georgia Sports Hall of Fame, Duane Allman's grave, Sidney Lanier's home, and Mrs. Robert E. Lee's rolling pin.

It also has 250,000 Yoshino cherry trees, about 10 times the number that glorify Washington, D.C.'s Tidal Basin. In late March the massed Yoshinos put a pretty pink frame around the city's landmarks and set the table for Macon's International Cherry Blossom Festival.

More than 500,000 visitors admire the Yoshinos' delicate pastel avalanche and take part in hundreds of events, most of them free. The agenda includes driving tours through downtown and the suburbs, all kinds of music, a children's program, a fancy dress ball, carnival rides, a golf tournament, bike and foot races, Frisbee competitions, cooking demonstrations, Japanese flower arranging, a hot-air-balloon festival, and parades of children and pets. Exhibits by a dozen or so countries lend the very Southern festival an international flair.

Prominent real estate developer William Fickling started the cherry blossom mania in the spring of 1952, when he discovered

Cherry Blossom Festival:

It may not have a Tidal Basin, but the annual late-March festival in Macon sports 10 times as many blossoms as Washington, D.C.

an exotic tree growing on his lawn. Its identity was a mystery until the following spring, when he saw his tree, in the thousands, lining Washington's Tidal Basin. It was the Yoshino, a fruitless cherry tree native to Japan.

Captivated by the tree's beauty, Fickling launched a campaign to make Macon perpetually pretty in pink. Up until his death in 1990, he donated 170,000 trees to neighborhoods, parks, and public and private buildings. A yearly giveaway program by Fickling's family increases the Yoshino population ever upward. First held in 1982 the Cherry Blossom Festival is one of the Southeast's premier annual events.

you know you're in
georgia when ...
... you're eating at Chick-fil-A

Chick-fil-A is a perfect example of how a really simple idea can get hold of people's imaginations. In the late 1950s S. Truett Cathy pressure-cooked a boneless chicken breast, sandwiched it between steamed buns with a couple of pickles, and put it on the menu of the Dwarf Grill in the south Atlanta suburb of Hapeville.

Airport workers and other Southsiders literally gobbled up the sandwich, and in 1967 Cathy opened the first eatery with the Chick-fil-A label in an Atlanta-area mall.

Word traveled fast, and so did the number of outlets—first in the Southeast, and then in the Southwest, Midwest, and across the Mississippi. These days, more than 1,300 locations in 36 states and Washington, D.C., make Chick-fil-A the second-largest chicken-based fast-food chain in the nation. The first waves were in shopping malls, but in recent years most of the growth has been in free-standing eateries with sit-down and drive-through service.

Like most successful enterprises, Chick-fil-A has thrived on catchy advertisements. "Eat Mor Chikin," the chain's ubiquitous slogan, features sign-wearing bovines that have united to reform American cuisine by reducing the amount of beef consumption.

Chick-fil-A:

Enjoy 'em every day but Sunday.

Chick-fil-A fans exercise their passion for chicken (available pressure-cooked, fried, or grilled in sandwiches, nuggets, wraps, salads, and breakfast biscuits) six days a week—but never on Sunday. Cathy's religious beliefs hold that even "chikins" need a day off.

...you're on the Georgia Peach's home turf

Tyrus Raymond Cobb summed up his philosophy thusly: "Baseball is a red-blooded sport for red-blooded men. It's no pink tea, and mollycoddles had better stay out. It's a struggle for supremacy, survival of the fittest."

Cobb grew up in Royston, in rural northeast Georgia. When he went off to play professional baseball in the early 1900s, his father, a school superintendent, newspaper publisher, and state legislator, warned him, "Don't come home a failure." Cobb kept that in his mind when he topped the .300 batting average in all but one of his 24 seasons in the major leagues, 22 of them with the Detroit Tigers and 2 with the Philadelphia Athletics.

Cobb's first great season was 1907, when he carried Detroit to the World Series with a .350 average, 212 hits, 119 RBIs, and 49 stolen bases. Starting that year, he won nine consecutive batting titles. His best years were 1911, when he led the American League in every major category except home runs and batted a career high .420, and 1915, when he stole 96 bases.

In his career Cobb compiled a .367 batting average, the highest in the history of the game. He hit safely 4,191 times and holds the record for 2,245 runs scored.

Along with his bat and glove, Cobb is best remembered for his intimidating style. He sharpened his spikes and came feet-first at opposing fielders. He used his fists on and off the field. Widely acknowledged as the greatest baseball player of all time, in 1936 he was the nearly unanimous first inductee to the Baseball Hall of Fame on the basis of his accomplishments on the field.

A terror on the field, "the Peach" had a soft spot. He helped fund Cobb Memorial Hospital in Royston, dedicated to his parents, and the Cobb Health Care System, with facilities in three northeast Georgia counties. He also endowed a college scholarship fund for worthy scholars.

The Ty Cobb Museum in Royston commemorates his feats with vintage equipment, photos, interviews, and a film with rare footage of Cobb in action.

Cobb, Ty:

This "Georgia Peach" fell from a tree in the small northeast Georgia town of Royston.

Coca-Cola is as Georgian as the Bulldogs, red clay, and sweet tea. The beverage began its journey to the international marketplace about 20 years after Appomattox. At his Columbus apothecary Dr. John Stith Pemberton concocted the syrup that would eventually evolve into the world's most famous soft drink. He took his formula to Atlanta in May 1886, carrying a jugful to Jacobs Pharmacy on Peachtree Street. According to Coke lore, it was "accidentally" blended with carbonated water instead of still water and pronounced "tasty" and "refreshing."

Pemberton's bookkeeper, Frank Robinson, reputedly came up with the name and coined the now-famous "Coca-Cola" script in his fine penmanship. Signs and flyers ballyhooed its taste and healthful qualities, but during the first year less than a dozen drinks a day were dispensed from the Jacobs soda fountain.

Enter Asa Candler, an Atlanta wholesale drug buyer who paid Pemberton $2,300 for sole ownership of Coca-Cola. A marketing wizard, Candler put the drink in wasp-waisted glass bottles, sold it in stores, and promoted sales with free drink coupons, souvenir fans, clocks, penknives, calendars, pocket watches, and other items.

During World War II Coke was provided to American troops all over the world. After the war the Coke empire spread to more than 200 countries, where more than a billion drinks are now enjoyed every day. The company's international headquarters is on North Avenue, a few blocks from the Varsity Drive-In, which reputedly sells more Coke than any other restaurant on the planet. The formula is as tightly guarded as the keys to Fort Knox.

The World of Coca-Cola is the company's show-off place. Coke World's self-guided tour takes more than a million visitors each year through the history of the drink, from Pemberton to the present. The facility is scheduled to move from its original location near the state capitol to a greatly expanded home near the Georgia Aquarium in summer 2007.

Coca-Cola:

Born in Atlanta, poured around the world.

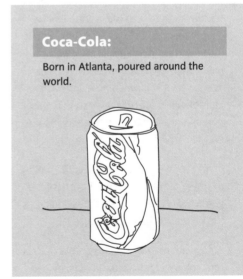

With 159 counties, Georgia has more jurisdictions than any state except Texas, which has 254 counties but is more than four times our size (261,914 square miles vs. 57,919). California, three times our size and population, has only 58 counties. Florida and Alabama, only a few square miles smaller than Georgia, get by with 67, the same as New York.

In the 19th century, when they apparently didn't have much else to do, the state's lawmakers decreed that it was every citizen's inalienable right to be within a half-day's horseback ride from the courthouse. That way all Georgians could do their voting, unhitch their spouses, sue their neighbors, etc., and ride home in time for supper before sundown.

Many of Georgia's counties are so small that you can toss a cow chip from one end to the other, and so thinly populated that you wouldn't hit anybody if you did. The tiniest rural counties have fewer than 2,000 citizens to support school systems, sheriffs, judges, social services, and other pillars of government.

The county mill kept churning well into the 1920s, when Model Ts were becoming the transportation of choice for many farm folks. The last county came online in 1924 when peach growers complained that there was a Bacon County and a Coffee County,

Counties:

With 159 of 'em, Georgia is second only to Texas.

but no county for the state's best-known crop. Peach County was created from the ribs of Macon and Houston Counties.

Georgia would have 161 counties, but Milton and Campbell bankrupted during the Great Depression and threw in with Atlanta's Fulton.

Officially, Georgia is nicknamed the Peach State, the Empire State of the South, and the Goober State (for its mother lode of peanuts). Unofficially, it's called the Cracker State. Historically, the name suggested poor, white, rural Southerners with little formal education.

In Elizabethan England, a Cracker was a loud-talking braggart. In the 1760s the English used the derogatory term to disparage Scots-Irish settlers in the Southern colonies. A letter from an English official in South Carolina to a colleague in New York reads: "I should explain to your Lordship what is meant by Crackers; a name they got from being great boasters; they are a lawless set of rascals on the frontiers of Virginia, Maryland, the Carolinas and Georgia, who often change their place of abode."

In the 19th century the term *cracker* was pinned on piney-woods Georgia and Florida cattle drovers, who cracked their whips to move their charges along. It also could have come from the practice of "cracking" corn to create potent, illegal liquor. As in the folk tune, "Jimmy cracked corn, and I don't care, my master's gone away. . . ."

Whatever the origin, many Georgians take perverse pride in being tagged a Cracker. For more than 60 years, the Atlanta Crackers were the New York Yankees of minor-league baseball, winning the Southern

Cracker:

When you call me that, smile.

Association pennant year after year, from 1901 to 1965. When the major-league Milwaukee Braves moved their franchise to Atlanta-Fulton County Stadium, the city no longer needed a minor-league team. However, some baseball fans hoped the Crackers nickname would live on.

To no avail, of course. But the name is not completely forgotten. Crackin' Good Snacks, owned by Southern grocery chain Winn-Dixie, produces Georgia Crackers, saltine-like crackers in a red tin with a picture of the Crescent, a Greek Revival home in Valdosta.

you know you're in
georgia when ...
... you're standing in the world's largest oil painting

It's colossal. It's dramatic. It's "As the War Turns." Cannons are firing, and men and horses are dying all around you. It's Atlanta's Cyclorama, supposedly the "longest continuously running show in the country." *Cats* and *Les Mis* don't even come close.

Created by German artists in Milwaukee in 1886, the 15,030-square-foot cylindrical painting is 42 feet tall and 358 feet in circumference, and it weighs 9,400 pounds. It depicts a successful attack by General William T. Sherman's Union forces on General John B. Hood's outnumbered Confederates on the outskirts of Atlanta on July 22, 1864. Sherman won the day, and Atlanta soon fell.

Diehard Rebels hail the valor of their boys in gray, but ironically, the painting was commissioned by Union Major General John A. "Blackjack" Logan to promote his candidacy for the U.S. Senate. Logan is depicted leading a counterattack.

Displayed in Grant Park since 1892, the painting was one of many oversize, circular paintings that once toured the country—a kind of 19th-century IMAX. The Depression-era Works Progress Administration added three-dimensional soldiers (Clark Gable's features are on one), trees, wagon wheels, cannon, and railroad tracks, all of which blend almost seamlessly into the scene.

The painting rotates as narration by James Earl Jones follows the action.

Civil War relics grace the lobby of the building that houses the Cyclorama. Among them are the steam engine *Texas,* which Confederates used to chase and capture Union raiders who had stolen the engine *General* at Kennesaw. The episode, known as the Great Locomotive Chase, is immortalized in a Walt Disney film by the same name.

Cyclorama:

The Battle of Atlanta still rages in the round.

you know you're in
georgia when...
...you visit the site of America's first gold rush

CNN wasn't there to record it, but it's a safe bet that when trapper Benjamin Parks first saw gold in the northeast Georgia hills, he didn't shout "Eureka! I have found it!" In amazement, he probably muttered something more like, "Well, goshdarn, would you look at that?"

What Parks unearthed near Dahlonega in 1828 was the beginning of America's first major gold rush. When word of his discovery reached the outside world, treasure hunters came running with their panning gear at the ready. Pretty soon miners were boring into the hillsides all around the rough-and-ready little town of Dahlonega, whose name was coined from the Cherokee word *talonega,* meaning "golden."

Some prospectors struck it rich; others left empty-handed. The real losers were the Cherokee, whose gold-rich lands were confiscated when they were exiled to Oklahoma on the Trail of Tears.

A branch of the United States Mint in Dahlonega cranked out about $6 million in gold coin denominations of $1.00, $2.50 (quarter eagle), $5.00 (half eagle), and $10.00 (eagle) from 1838 until 1861, when it was captured by Confederate troops. The Treasury Department didn't reactivate the mint after Appomattox, so numismatists put a high premium on any Dahlonega coins that surface these days.

When the mint building burned in 1878, North Georgia College built Price Memorial Hall on the foundation and topped it with a landmark gold leaf spire. The gold leaf on the state capitol dome in Atlanta is periodically redone with Dahlonega gold.

There's still gold in these here hills, most of it in the pockets of tourists who come to Dahlonega to pan at commercial camps and explore once-lucrative mines. The Gold Museum in the town square tells the gold rush story and exhibits coins and nuggets.

There's also wine in these hills. Three vineyards and wineries a short drive from the square attract oenophiles, some of whom may shout "Eureka!" when they sip a chardonnay or a pinot noir at Wolf Mountain, Three Sisters, or Frogtown Cellars.

Dahlonega Gold:

Benjamin Parks accidentally stumbled onto a good thing.

you know you're in
georgia when...
...you're in the Carpet Capital of the World

If you have carpeting on your floor, chances are excellent that it came from Dalton, which bills itself as the Carpet Capital of the World. Mills in Dalton and a 65-mile radius thereabouts produce the goods for 80 percent of the U.S. carpet market, which supplies 45 percent of the world market.

Dalton gained eminence largely thanks to the automobile. In the early 1900s, Dixie Highway, one of Georgia's first paved roads, 120 miles between Chattanooga and Atlanta, ran through rural areas of northwest Georgia. This thoroughfare gave women the chance to make extra money selling bedspreads, which they hung on clotheslines by the roadway.

The women used a technique called "candlewick embroidery," which dated back to the 18th century and employed white cords that resembled candle wicks. By far the most popular design featured two peacocks with colorful tail feathers. Jesus Christ, floral patterns, and the Confederate battle flag were also big sellers. You might want to check out grandma's trunk up there in the attic. Sold for a dollar or less, the surviving originals now sell to collectors for hundreds, sometimes thousands, of dollars.

In the mid-1920s the government built U.S. Highway 41, modern for the times, which brought more and more travelers through what was nicknamed Peacock Alley.

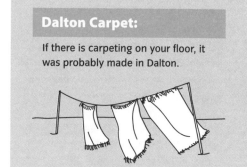

Dalton Carpet:

If there is carpeting on your floor, it was probably made in Dalton.

In the 1930s Catherine Evans Whitener turned the popular tufting technique into a small industry. She and her brother built a mill where local women semi-mass-produced hand-tufted bedspreads. Other hand-tufters followed suit, organizing "spread houses." By the end of the Depression, labor-intensive hand-tufting was converted to machines. Then, after World War II the machines used to tuft bedspreads were converted to manufacture carpets. Wall-to-wall carpeting, popular in postwar homes, sent carpet sales skyrocketing, and the billion-dollar industry was on its way.

Today, more than 100 plants and outlets line U.S. 41 from Adairsville, north of Dalton, to Calhoun and Cartersville to the south. At Crown Gardens and Archives, in Dalton's original manufacturing plant, guides demonstrate how bedspreads were tufted and how they evolved into a vital industry.

you know you're in
georgia when...
...you remember when Paula Deen was a Bag Lady

Hostess of a popular network TV show, author of a slew of cookbooks, publisher of her own magazine, proprietor of Savannah's most famous restaurant, and fledgling Hollywood actress, Paula Deen started her road to success with Saran-wrapped tuna sandwiches.

Plagued with agoraphobia (fear of the open, public places), newly divorced with two small boys to feed, and with only $200 between her and homelessness, Deen cashed in an asset from her Southern heritage. She knew how to feed hungry folks, so in 1989 she launched The Bag Lady, a business that delivered sandwiches to construction crews and offices around Savannah. She stayed home and made the sandwiches her sons went out to sell.

Two years later, with the Bag Lady outgrowing her kitchen, Deen overcame her phobia and opened The Lady in Savannah's southside suburbs. Her wizardry with fried chicken, collard greens, and other culinary icons prompted her to open The Lady and Sons in downtown Savannah's City Market. From day one, crowds lined up for their chance to sample Deen's cornucopial buffet.

In 2003 the restaurant moved down the street, into a three-story former warehouse with four times the seating. With the success of *Paula's Home Cooking* on the Food

Deen, Paula:

Julia Child with a sweet-tea accent.

Network, which made its debut in November 2002, and Deen's appearances on *Oprah,* crowds wait in even longer lines at the new space.

In 2005 Deen made her Hollywood debut in *Elizabethtown,* in which she played—you'd never guess—Orlando Bloom's Aunt Dora, a folksy Southern cook. She had a high old time, preparing hoecakes and other Southern goods for the cast and crew. "That Kirsten Dunst is as cute as a pig's ear," Deen gushed, in typical Southernese, about the movie's co-star.

You're welcome to stop by The Lady and Sons at 102 West Congress Street (912–233–2600). Get there early, you heah?

you know you're in
georgia when ...
... you're on *Deliverance* River

In 1972 four city slickers from Atlanta took an R & R raft trip down the wild and crazy Chattooga River in northeast Georgia. Their vehicle was John Boorman's film *Deliverance,* taken from the pages of South Carolinian James Dickey's adventure novel.

Churning over the Chattooga's hell-for-leather rapids, the quartet—Burt Reynolds, Jon Voight, Ned Beatty, and Ronny Cox—found more outdoor adventure than they could handle, all tangled up with violence, murder, and mayhem.

They also exposed the outside world to one of Georgia's best-kept secrets. Flowing through a crease in the Blue Ridge Mountains—past hillsides thick with rhododendron, mountain laurel, and many species of ferns, not to mention otters, bears, and beavers—are the Chattooga's Class 4 and Class 5 rapids. Squeezed through walls of rock and stomach-turning sluices, they are a challenge to experienced rafters and were far beyond the abilities of Reynolds & Company—and of the thousands of greenhorn moviegoers who bought themselves rafts or truck inner tubes and set off to "do" the Chattooga on their own.

After many were injured and several were killed, Congress in 1974 designated the Chattooga a "Wild and Scenic River," under protection of the U.S. Forestry Service (USFS). The USFS licenses professional outfitters to conduct river rides in sturdy six-person rubber rafts led by guides who know every rapid, rock, and rill along the tempestuous waterway.

Beginners usually test their courage on Section III, a seven-hour, 6-mile ride that sweeps them through many *Deliverance* landmarks. Section IV is the "ultimate challenge," a rip-snorting, seven-hour white-knuckler through swiftly moving currents; up steep gorges; and up and over, down and around such perils as Seven Foot Falls, Bull Sluice, Corkscrew, and Jawbone.

At day's end, the Chattooga finally turns you loose at a peaceful stretch of shoreline or into the calm waters of Tugaloo Lake. Whew! Can we go back and do that again?

Deliverance River:

Burt and Jon's little ride sent the world running to the Chattooga.

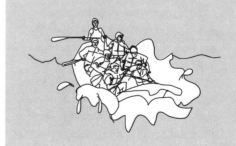

you know you're in
georgia when...
...you're doing the Dirty Bird

The "Dirty Bird" is an arm-flapping dance that celebrated the Atlanta Falcons' once-and-only glorious season. In 1998, when the city's NFL team was bound for the biggest year since its birth in 1966, running back Jamal Anderson scored a touchdown that iced a 41–0 win over the New England Patriots. Anderson—who would finish the season with 14 touchdowns and 1,846 rushing yards—was so elated by his feat that he began hopping around the end zone, extending his arms and raising his elbows.

Caught up in the excitement, 70,000 fans in the Georgia Dome began hopping up and down and flapping with him, until the entire stadium looked like a giant birdcage about to take flight. Questioned by a reporter, Anderson called his creation the Dirty Bird, and the Falcons themselves became known around the league as the Dirty Birds.

According to the Falcons' Web site, the dance goes like this: (1) Hop to the right with your elbows raised. (2) Hop to the left and jerk your right elbow down, as if you're pulling on something. (3) Hop to the right and extend your left elbow away from your body. (4) Hop to the left and extend your left elbow away from your body. At this point your elbows should be back in their original raised position. Now flap your wings like a bird, and at the same time hop back and forth until you're tired.

The "Birds" danced to a 14–2 record, beat the Minnesota Vikings in the NFC championship game, and went onto Super Bowl XXIII, where John Elway and the Denver Broncos clipped their wings. Anderson suffered a season-ending knee injury in game two of the 1999 season, and without his inspiration the Dirty Birds finished a dismal 5–11. The Super Bowl has evaded them ever since.

Like the Macarena, the Lambada, and the Hokey Pokey, the Dirty Bird is an almost-forgotten page of Falcon history. When the scoreboard exhorts fans in the Georgia Dome to "Do the Dirty Bird," only a handful of fans who "remember when," remember how.

The Dirty Bird:

Some loyal Atlanta Falcons fans hope to flap their team to another Super Bowl.

you know you're in
georgia when...
...you know Mark Trail

Mark Trail is a forever-30, ruggedly hand-some outdoorsman who lives with his wife, Cherry, adopted son, Rusty, and faithful St. Bernard, Andy, in the Lost Forest National Park, Somewhere-in-the-U.S.A. He's been enjoying the great outdoors and working for the preservation of the natural environment since April 15, 1946, when Georgia native Ed Dodd created him as a daily comic-strip character in the *New York Post*.

Born in LaFayette, in northwest Georgia in 1902, Dodd was sketching, drawing, and painting practically as soon as he got out of diapers. In the 1920s he spent his summers working at a Pennsylvania boys' camp run by Dan Beard, a founder of the Boy Scouts of America. Dodd then taught physical education in Gainesville (Georgia) schools; briefly attended Georgia Tech, where he illustrated the yearbook; and fell in love with the American West while working on a Wyoming dude ranch.

In 1930 he drew a humorous, family-life strip in the *Atlanta Journal*. But the West and the outdoors dominated his imagination. The *New York Post* went for his concept of an outdoorsman whom Dodd originally called Jim Tree.

Renamed *Mark Trail*, the series—which was syndicated in hundreds of American and foreign newspapers—revolved around its title character, an outdoorsman, writer, and

Dodd, Ed:

This Georgia native created Mark Trail, a forever-30, tree-hugging comic-strip conservationist.

photographer modeled after Dodd himself. Until 1983, when smoking started to become socially unacceptable, Trail was often drawn with a pipe in his mouth.

Dodd was named Honorary Chairman of National Wildlife Week in 1952–53 and Georgia Conservationist of the Year in 1967. He retired from writing *Mark Trail* in 1978 but passed the strip over to a longtime assistant who continues Trail's adventures into the 21st century.

Dodd died in May 1991 in Gainesville, where he promoted his conservation philosophy through the ongoing Mark Trail/Ed Dodd Foundation. A permanent exhibit on the cartoonist and his creation is at Gainesville's Brenau University.

Where do all the tombstones come from? An awful lot of them come from the Granite Capital of the World, northeast Georgia's Elbert County, where more than 40 quarries and 150 finishing plants send the blue-gray stone to every state and several foreign countries. Now a billion-dollar industry, Elbert County granite had a bizarre coming-out.

In 1898 the first finishing plant was built for the sole purpose of fashioning a Confederate soldier for Elberton's Public Square. But when the 7-foot Johnny Reb, standing on a 15-foot pedestal, was unveiled, townsfolk's Rebel yells turned to tears and jeers.

His moon face, squatty legs, and a uniform that looked suspiciously Union prompted wiseacres to say that he was "a cross between a Pennsylvania Dutchman and a hippopotamus" and derisively dub him Dutchy. Resentment built and finally boiled over in 1900, when a mob pulled him down from his perch, "lynched" him, and buried him face down, a military sign of disgrace.

The *Elberton Star* gleefully reported: "Dutchy is no more. The man with the stony glare took a tumble Monday night and now is lying in the middle of the square with two broken limbs. Dutchy had been feeling poorly for some time. He had a bad case of gout, judging from the size of his feet and legs, and he was compelled to wear a

Dutchy:

Alas, poor Dutchy, we hardly knew ye.

heavy United States Army overcoat, like Confederate soldiers didn't wear during the Civil War, and the hot weather got next to him."

Poor Dutchy was buried in Public Square, where a more pleasing Confederate trooper took his place on the pedestal.

Forgotten for eight decades, Dutchy was exhumed in 1982, run through a pressurized car wash, and, in recognition of his pioneering status, given a place of honor in the Elberton Granite Museum and Exhibit. All those decades in Georgia red clay had not diminished his finely crafted features.

...some of the best-named towns have gone extinct

Gone and mostly forgotten are many of the most colorful place-names that once graced our state map.

Blueshin, in Dougherty County, resembled a swollen foreleg. Booger Bottom, now on the bottom of Lake Lanier (aka Lake Sidney Lanier), was an old name for a place where hobgoblins dwelt. Box Ankle, a Monroe County village, got its name when two men got into fisticuffs at a cock fight and one was knocked over a wooden box and broke his ankle.

Cement, in Bartow County, died with its namesake industry. Cheap, in Washington County, priced itself out of existence. Dashboard, in Carroll County, memorialized the time Slick Chalmers's mule kicked the dashboard out of Cecil Spruell's new Model T. Fillmore, in Whitfield County, went the way of our 13th president, Millard (1850–1853). Likewise Garfield, in Emanuel County, which died not long after President James's 1881 assassination.

Hardscrabble, in Fulton County, was named for poor folks who had a hard time scrabbling a living from small farms. The name vanished long ago, and now the area is one of metro Atlanta's most affluent neighborhoods. Corporate CEOs and sports and entertainment celebs here have to hardscrabble to make the payments on Beemers, Jags, and multimillion-dollar McMansions.

Hopeulikit, in Bulloch County, was the name exasperated citizens hoped the post office would like after rejecting many others. Happily, the post office did "likit." Ditto for Nameless, in Laurens County. After Iceberg, in Monroe County, failed to live up to its name (there were no icebergs), it was changed to Juliette, the name of a local woman. (The town was the site of the Whistle Stop Cafe in the movie *Fried Green Tomatoes*.)

Tallapoosa, in Haraslon County (itself a sort of odd name), thankfully changed its name from Possum Snout. Tax, in Talbot County, was rescinded a century ago. Still alive and well, Enigma, in Berrien County, got its name when townsfolk reckoned it was a puzzlement why they couldn't come up with a name for their town. There's no riddle to Riddlesville, in Washington County, which honors a bygone landowner.

Extinct Towns:

Gone, and happily forgotten. (Well, most at least.)

WELCOME TO ICEBERG JULIETTE

Fall foliage in New England and other northerly places is dead and buried under snow and ice by the time the hardwoods in northern Georgia break out in scarlet, orange, yellow, and gold. In late October and early November, when our meteorologists give the signal that the leaves are at their dazzling peak, highways headed north from Atlanta and other cities are jammed with "leaf lookers."

The Russell-Brasstown Scenic Byway in Union and White Counties takes you through the heart of northeast Georgia's most spectacular fall foliage. The 14-mile highway (Highway 348) begins at the edge of the Alpine-themed village of Helen, crosses the Appalachian Trail at 3,137-foot Tesnatee Gap, and continues on toward 4,784-foot Brasstown Bald, the state's highest mountain.

Dahlonega, where America's first gold rush took place in the late 1820s, is a good place to stop. There you can pan for gold and enjoy family-style cooking at the famous Smith House before heading northeast on U.S. Highway 19 to Vogel State Park, or northwest on Highway 52 to Amicalola Falls State Park, site of the state's highest, most accessible waterfall.

Other scenic routes include Highway 197 north from Clarkesville. If you choose it, stop at the Mark of the Potter, a former grist mill, to admire the artistry of north Georgia potters and feed the fat trout in the rapids of the Soque River. U.S. Highway 76 is a scenic drive across the top of the state between Blue Ridge and Clayton. Old U.S. Highway 441 in Rabun and Habersham Counties passes two jewel-like lakes.

The hills are abuzz with fall festivals. For a change of pace from driving, ride a pontoon boat, canoe, or kayak on one of north Georgia's scenic lakes. It's a peaceful, quiet, and reflective time to enjoy the brisk mountain air, the autumn sunshine, and the brilliant north Georgia foliage.

Fall Foliage:

The hardwoods in northern Georgia are in their splendor long after the autumn glory in more northern locations has turned glacial.

32

you know you're in
georgia when...
...you're at the Fire Ant Festival

Even ardent nature lovers have a hard time finding something positive to say about fire ants. They're evil little demons, with no redeeming social value. About the same size and color as ordinary house and garden ants, they pack the venomous wallop of much larger yellow jackets, wasps, and hornets.

Step on one of their dome-shape mounds and you're in for it. They attack, en masse with a vengeful fury. They go after humans, cattle, whatever infringes on their turf. They can make you sick and can even be fatal. They're believed to have hitched shipboard rides from South America and embarked in the southern United States around 1918, from whence they quickly spread across much of the country.

South Georgia's farmlands and forests are especially bedeviled, and hospitals in the area treat dozens of cases yearly. Nonetheless, the town of Ashburn in Turner County puts on a Fire Ant Festival the fourth weekend of every March. Events include a parade with folks dressed up as their nemesis. There's also a pet parade, fun runs, a street dance, and a Strawberry Cookoff, with festivalgoers given the chance to sample the entries.

Fire Ant Festival:

Don't step on the honored guests.

The Fire Ant Calling Contest is one of the most popular events. How do you call a fire ant? "Any way you want," advises the Turner County Chamber of Commerce. And if they answer? "You're in a whole heap o' trouble."

The directors of the Folk Pottery Museum of Northeast Georgia claim that it's one of a kind. Some folk museums exhibit pottery as part of their overall collections, but the Georgia institution is, the directors believe, the only one dedicated exclusively to pottery.

The museum, which opened in fall 2006, is located in the picturesque northeast Georgia mountain community of Sautee Nacoochee. It showcases the workmanship of the state's potters from the early 1800s to the present. The 3,200-square-foot museum and a majority of its permanent collection were a gift from northeast Georgia residents Dean and Kay Swanson.

Initially, the Swansons had a small pottery collection. In 1999 they took the suggestion of a local artist and purchased an important 40-piece collection that became the foundation of the more than 150 pieces they've donated to the museum.

Families from the Carolinas brought the tradition of ash- and lime-glazed stoneware to northeast Georgia in the 1820s. Among the most celebrated potters are the late Cheever Meaders and his son, Lanier Meaders. From the late 1960s to his death in 1998, Lanier became internationally famous for his face jugs, which include a jowly Richard Nixon series. The Smithsonian Institution hailed Lanier as one of America's most outstanding folk artists.

Folk Pottery Museum:

Home to face jugs, five-spout wedding jugs, and other decorative clay objects created by nearly two centuries of Georgia mountain artists.

Originally crafted by South Carolina slaves, face jugs—also known as "ugly jugs"—have grotesque "haint" faces intended to scare children and others away from the whiskey stored inside.

One of the rarest pieces in the museum is a five-spout wedding jug from the 1870s. A bridesmaid carried the jug, filled with flowers, during the wedding ceremony. At the reception the flowers were tossed and the jug was filled with strong drink; the bride, groom, maid of honor, and best man drank from the spouts around the edge. The spout in the center was for the preacher, who maintained his abstinence lest the drink spill all over his shirt front.

you know you're in
georgia when...
...you see Atlanta's First Lady

If Atlanta had a First Lady, her name would probably be Jane. Fonda, that is. Daughter of Henry, brother of Peter, and aunt of Bridget, she's been an A-list activist since she was old enough to know right from left. In the 1960s she campaigned for civil rights and against the Vietnam War. In 1972 she went to Hanoi and got labeled a traitor; she belatedly apologized, but war veterans and others won't accept it.

Fonda won her first of six Best Actress Golden Globes in 1962, for *Walk on the Wild Side*. Two Best Actress Oscars followed, one in 1971 for *Klute* and another in 1978 for *Coming Home,* the story of a disabled Vietnam War vet's difficult readjustment to civilian life.

In 1981 Fonda achieved a long-held wish to play opposite her estranged father. For his role as her father in *On Golden Pond,* Henry won his only Best Actor Oscar. In 2005 Fonda ended 14 years of retirement with the box office success *Monster-in-Law,* which costarred Jennifer Lopez and premiered at Atlanta's Fox Theater.

In 1991 Fonda married Atlanta's own Ted Turner. When they divorced 10 years later, she became a full-time Atlanta resident. In 2002 she established the Jane Fonda Center for Adolescent Reproductive Health at Emory University to help prevent teenage pregnancy and promote women's reproductive rights.

In 2006 a roast in Fonda's honor attracted former president Jimmy Carter, Debbie Reynolds, Rosie O'Donnell, Larry King, and ex-husband Ted.

Fonda, Jane:

Actress, activist, and honorary First Lady of Atlanta.

Imagine, on Christmas Day, 1929, taking a streetcar to the corner of Peachtree Street and Ponce de Leon Avenue, where squat onion domes and towering minarets rose like an Arabian Nights mirage among Victorian houses and scattered retail shops. Imagine buying tickets at the brass kiosk made in France, strolling the grand entrance arcade, passing through the carpeted lobby and into the vast auditorium, and gazing up at the blue-painted ceiling, twinkling with electric stars and drifting clouds.

Seven years after the discovery of Tutankhamen's tomb, the craze for everything Egyptian was echoed in the Fox Theater. Scarabs of the Egyptian sun god and likenesses of Tut and his wife and Queen Nefertiti graced murals, ceilings, powder room chairs, ash receptacles, and theater seats. Those motifs blended harmoniously with Moorish arches and balconies and other Oriental features.

After the spectacular architecture, the movie could only be an anticlimax. But the live "warm-ups" held up their end. A 3,610-pipe Moller organ cranked out a medley of classical and popular music, a full orchestra played, and a troupe of leggy dancers took the stage—all before the screen lit up for *Steamboat Willie*, Walt Disney's first Mickey Mouse cartoon. Then came the feature film: *Salute*, a "talkie" comedy with Stepin Fetchit.

Originally built as a Shriners temple—which explains the Oriental design—the theater opened only two months after the Wall Street crash of 1929 and soon was bought by the Fox Pictures Corporation, which kept the house packed with first-run movies through the Great Depression and World War II, into the 1950s and early 1960s. In the 1970s television, suburban flight, and drive-ins led to the Fox's decline.

The theater closed in 1975, seemingly destined for a date with a wrecking ball. But in the nick of time, leaders of a "Save the Fox" campaign bought and restored the theater to its original glory as a venue for everything from Broadway musicals to summertime movie festivals.

Fox Theater:

Still fabulous after nearly 80 years.

Fruitcakes and the annual Rattlesnake Roundup are the hallmarks of Claxton, a town of 2,600 deep in southeast Georgia.

Which came first? It was fruitcakes, by six decades. In 1910 Italian immigrant Sovino Tos opened a bakery that flooded the little farming town with the aromas of baking bread, pastries, homemade ice cream, and fruitcake. Although fruitcake—which contains dried and candied fruit and nuts and is doused with rum or bourbon—is associated with the South at Christmastime, it was actually an ancient Roman delicacy made with pomegranate seeds, fruit, pine nuts, and raisins. Tos's modern version of the old Italian cake made his reputation and kept his bakery open through the Great Depression and World War II.

After the war Tos sold his bakery to his assistant, Albert Parker, who decided to specialize solely in fruitcake. In its first year of mass production, Parker's Claxton Bakery produced 45,000 pounds of fruitcake. Production soared as the bakery's reputation spread the demand around the country and overseas. In the 1950s Parker began selling his cakes through civic clubs as fund-raisers, cementing Claxton's eminence as the Fruitcake Capital of the World. It says so right on the town's water tower.

The Claxton Rattlesnake Roundup began in 1968 when a local farm boy, David Wiggins,

Fruitcakes and Rattlesnakes:

Even in Claxton, they're never served on the same plate.

was bitten by an eastern diamondback rattler. He survived, but the incident focused attention on the dangers of venomous snakes. So every March since then, the Evans County Rattlesnake Roundup turns the hunt for vipers into a country fair, with marching bands, beauty queens, amusement park rides, barbecue and funnel cakes, and arts and crafts. Prizes are given for the biggest, fattest, and largest number of snakes bagged by a hunting team.

Supporters point out that antivenin from the snakes helps save the lives of victims. Conservationists counter that snakes are an important part of the environment and that some methods used to round them up are harmful to gopher tortoises and other protected endangered species.

you know you're in
georgia when...
...you hear *Funeral of the Air* on AM radio

Although they're disappearing, *The County Hospital Report* and *Funeral of the Air* can still be heard on a few rural Georgia AM radio stations. Sponsored by the local hospital, the announcer reads the names of patients currently admitted, with their ailments, their condition, and those who've recently come to wish them well.

A typical report might go like this: "Mrs. Judith (Judy) Traherne of Lumber City was admitted to Jeff Davis County Hospital on Friday with pneumonia. Mrs. Traherne is being cared for by Jeff Davis Hospital's caring staff and is doing much better. On Sunday she was visited by her husband, Roscoe Traherne; her sister, Miss Charlotte Vale of Boston, Georgia; her children and grandchildren; the choir of Resurrection is the Life Church, where she sings soprano; and several friends and neighbors."

If all that visiting proves fatal, Mrs. Traherne will be featured on *Funeral of the Air,* sponsored by the local mortuary. With an organ playing somberly in the background, a mortician with a voice like old-time radio's Digger O'Dell tolls the sad news of Mrs. Traherne's passing and invites her many friends to the viewing Wednesday night and funeral services Thursday morning at Autumn Leaves Mortuary, caring for your loved ones since 1957.

Funeral of the Air:

AM radio's down-home reality show.

Some AM stations also broadcast daily school cafeteria menus and the names of absentees, in case those listening want to change their minds and come in for Jell-O and Sloppy Joes.

Herbert Hoover's 1920s electioneering promise of "a chicken in every pot" is fulfilled every day in Gainesville and elsewhere in north Georgia.

In the early 1900s chickens were largely a "cottage industry," with the birds raised primarily for their eggs. That changed dramatically in the 1930s, when Gainesville feed salesman Jesse Jewell made farmers a proverbial deal that they couldn't refuse. He'd sell them baby chicks and feed on credit. When the chicks were grown, his company would buy the adult chickens (broilers) at a price that would cover his costs and guarantee farmers a profit.

Jewell invested his capital in a processing plant and hatchery. The addition of a feed mill and rendering plant in the mid-1950s completed the vertical integration of his company into a production line similar to an automobile assembly plant.

After World War II it seemed like everybody in north Georgia was getting into the chicken business. By 1995 Georgia annually processed more than 5 billion pounds of chickens. Three years later, it became the top broiler-producing state in the country, a rank it has held ever since.

A monument on Jesse Jewell Parkway, in downtown Gainesville's Poultry Park, hails the city as "The cradle of the poultry industry, inseparately linked since WWII, when pioneering efforts by the industry's greatest names transformed the 'barnyard hen' into the First Lady of industrial agriculture and turned the eyes of the world toward Gainesville as the cradle and capital of the modern poultry industry...."

As for that eternal question, "Which came first?" scientists say that it was neither the chicken nor the egg. They declare that reptiles were laying eggs millions of years before chickens evolved. Chickens, the scientists have determined, are the closest living relatives of the *Tyrannosaurus rex*.

Which brings the question back full circle.

Gainesville Poultry:

Enough chickens for every pot on earth.

you know you're in
georgia when...
...you need a phrase book to understand the natives

Traveling around the state, you're naturally going to want to stop and converse with the inhabitants. But as is the case in any foreign country, you're sometimes going to hit a language barrier. Here are a few helpful hints to get you over the rough spots.

When Georgians say they're "fixin'" to do something, it doesn't necessarily mean they're repairing something. Instead, they're studying on it, or working up the steam to get around to it.

"That dog don't hunt" isn't meant to dispute a canine's lack of interest in a foray in the woods. It's a polite way of saying, "I question the veracity of that last remark."

"High as a Georgia pine" is a colorful way of announcing that mama's been in the cooking sherry again. And "so good you'll slap your granny" is another way of saying, "Emeril and Wolfgang, eat your heart out."

If someone says that you're "all vine and no taters," better change your attitude. It means that you're a braggart with nothing to brag about. Especially if you keep talking about how things are done up North. Go too far on that track, and locals will respond, "Delta is ready when you are."

When somebody puts on a big smile and declares, "Y'all come see us real soon, you heah?" don't take it as an invitation to Sunday dinner. It's like saying, "Good to see you." Maybe they think so; maybe they don't. And when people ask, "How you doin'?" they actually don't want to know about your recent bout of pneumonia.

Some phrases are plenty colorful without being hard to interpret. Among them: "This weather's so dry, you have to prime yourself before you expectorate" and "That ol' boy was born tired and growed up lazy."

Georgia Lingo:

State natives have their own colorful way of talkin'.

...a local stone is too "marble-ous" for words

Pickens County, in northeast Georgia, is the home of the state's only major marble quarry. Native Americans, notably Creek and Cherokee, created religious icons and other items from marble as early as A.D. 800.

Early white settlers came looking for gold, but they also found silver, graphite, aquamarine, and other precious substances. In the early 1830s a young man named Henry Fitzsimmons made an extremely valuable discovery: one of the world's largest deposits of exceptionally pure pink Etowah marble. It ran 5 to 7 miles long, ½ mile wide, and 2,000 feet deep. Fitzsimmons built the first marble mill and in the 1880s established the Georgia Marble Company, in what is now the little town of Tate.

When the railroad connected Pickens County with the outside world, the pink-hued stone was shipped across the country and used in numerous public and private buildings. In Washington, D.C., Georgia marble beautifies the Lincoln memorial, the U.S. House and Senate office buildings, and the East Wing of the National Gallery of Art.

In the early 1900s Colonel Sam Tate took over the operations of Georgia Marble. His legacy includes the all-marble Tate Elementary School (in the town named for him), the only such school in the United States. His home, the Tate House Mansion, built in

Georgia Marble:

The pink Etowah stone graces buildings from coast to coast.

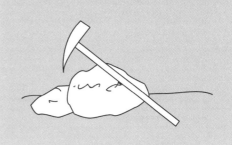

1926, has been restored to its original grandeur with marble floors, mantles, and bathroom fixtures plus 27 acres of gardens. It's a popular place for weddings and other special events.

If you'd like to see the quarry, come to the Georgia Marble Festival in early October, the only time the quarry is open to the public. Parades, arts and crafts, and other fun stuff goes on, too.

you know you're in
georgia when...
...you can visit Ray Charles and Alan Jackson in one stop

What if you could put Ray Charles, Travis Tritt, Trisha Yearwood, Alan Jackson, Johnny Mercer, opera diva Jessye Norman, the Allman Brothers Band, bandleader Harry James, Otis Redding, "Little Richard" Penniman, Ronnie Milsap, "Godfather of Soul" James Brown, and more than 100 other Georgia-born musicians all in one big room?

The Georgia Music Hall of Fame in downtown Macon has accomplished that seemingly impossible feat.

The "musical village" takes you on a stroll through the Peach State's amazingly diverse musical heritage. You can sit in small theaters and watch videos of gospel, pop, rock, swing, big band, and country artists and tune in to your favorites on headphones around the museum.

Aside from the pure enjoyment, the Hall of Fame is a learning experience. Even if they didn't know it before Jamie Foxx's Oscar-winning role in the 2004 biopic *Ray,* most everybody knows by now that Ray Charles was born in Albany, where he lived until he was about five or six years old. Country music fans are well aware that Tritt was born in Marietta and Yearwood in Monticello, and opera fans are familiar with Norman's rise from the choir at an Augusta church to the stage of the Metropolitan and La Scala.

Georgia Music Hall of Fame:

Ray Charles, Harry James, Trisha Yearwood, and Jessye Norman. How's that for a musical ensemble?

But who knew that swing bandleader Harry James was born in 1916 in Albany, where his father, the bandleader of a traveling circus, taught him the trumpet? James moved to Texas in 1931, from whence he went to New York and formed his own band in 1939. Four years later he became the envy of American troops in the Atlantic and Pacific when he married their pinup dream girl, Betty Grable.

Most of the musicographies are a quick study, but you'll have to be familiar with Braille to read blind country music star Milsap's June 1995 issue of *Playboy.*

you know you're in
georgia when...
...being understood is all in the pronunciation

When Jimmy Carter was elected president, Georgians were delighted that we finally had a chief executive without an accent. Being understood often requires a conversational partner with the ability to decipher seemingly "foreign" sounds.

If Juan Ponce de Leon showed up in Atlanta, he wouldn't know his own name. The 16th-century Spaniard, who came to Florida seeking the Fountain of Youth, has the same moniker as a thoroughfare that begins at Spring Street in midtown and courses for more than 20 miles through the suburbs. But if he asked a native, "¿Donde esta Ponce de Leon Avenue?" with the proper Castillian pronunciation ("Pon-cey de lay-on"), the native would stare, tilt his/her head right and left, and profess ignorance of any such street.

In Atlanta-ese, the avenue is known as "Pawntz duh Lee-awn." It got its name from a spring that once flowed under what is now the massive brick hulk of City Hall East. The spring was named, you guessed it, after the explorer.

By the way, only newcomers pronounce the second *t* in Atlanta. To us it's "At-lanna." Away from the capital city, Marietta is "May-retta," Cairo is "Kay-ro," Vienna is "VIE-enna," and Albany is "All-benny." The counties of Houston and Taliaferro are "House-ton" and "Toll-i-ver," respectively.

As for more practical objects: A "tar" is one of the round things that keeps your car rolling, as in, "I run over a nail and got a flat tar." A "spire" is what you keep in your trunk in case of a flat tar.

"Farn" and "furriner" are somebody not from around here, like Miss'sippi or Flawda. "Shivalay" is an unfarn car.

A "camry" is what you take pitchers with. And "dite" is what to do when you've overet.

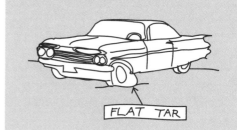

Georgia Pronunciations:
Could you say that again, real slow?

FLAT TAR

you know you're in
georgia when ...
... you cross the Gnat Line

Driving south of Macon on a steamy, hot summer day, you innocently get out for a pit stop, and you're immediately besieged by a blitzkrieg of tiny predators.

You've crossed the Gnat Line, my friends, an insect Maginot Line that separates the state's hilly Piedmont Plateau from the flat, buggy Coastal Plain. The *New World Dictionary* defines gnats as "any of various unrelated two-winged insects, some of which bite or sting."

They apparently bedeviled biblical folk, as well. In Matthew 23-24, Christ accused judges of "straining at a gnat," or making mountains out of molehills.

However, you define 'em, whammo!, they're on you like white on rice. They hit you in the face, wage all-out war on your eyes, ears, and nasal passages. They sting any exposed flesh, bore right through clothing. They chase you back to your vehicle like Sheriff Jackie Gleason highballing after Burt Reynolds in *Smokey and the Bandit*.

In high-gnat season, which is pretty much any time the temperature is above freezing, normally chatty natives south of the Gnat Line are more close-mouthed than normal, lest a stem-winding yarn become an open-door invitation to tonsillar invasion.

Gnats are especially vicious in swampy places like the Okefenokee and the coastal islands, and in midsummer they may be your most lasting impression of gracious Savannah and balmy Jekyll Island.

As they say down here, if you can't beat 'em, throw 'em a party. The little kamikazes are honored guests at Camilla's Gnat Day, the first weekend of May.

The Gnat Line:

You won't need a signpost to tell you when you've crossed this boundary.

After the Civil War, when Atlanta claimed the state capital as spoils of war from Milledgeville, the lawmakers met for nearly two decades in an opera house, school buildings, and other venues. When they appropriated $1 million in 1883 to build a proper capitol, the enabling legislation specified that "all materials used in construction of said building shall be those found and procured within the state of Georgia; provided that same can be procured in said state as cheaply as other materials of like quality in other states."

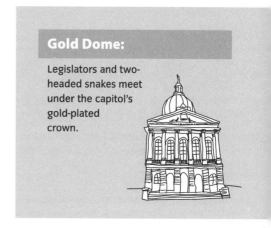

Gold Dome:

Legislators and two-headed snakes meet under the capitol's gold-plated crown.

Try as it might to comply, the building commission discovered that it was cheaper to import Indiana limestone for the exterior than to obtain granite and marble from then-undeveloped north Georgia quarries. The commission redeemed the embarrassment when the building was completed on time.

Seventy-five years later, the state's own resources were finally put into play. Originally sheathed in tin, the surface of the capitol dome was covered with 43 ounces of gold donated to the state by the citizens of Dahlonega and Lumpkin County.

A wagon train brought the gold from Dahlonega, some 60 miles away, in August 1958. When weather took its toll on the gold, wagon trains brought a fresh supply in 1979 and again in 1998. Residents of Lumpkin County are already panning their mountain streams for a new batch to be applied in 2018.

Above the dome, a 15-foot-tall "Miss Freedom" holds aloft a torch symbolizing freedom and commemorating the state's war casualties. In the interior rotunda, which rises to 237 feet, busts and portraits in the Georgia Hall of Fame honor America's Founding Fathers, state signers of the Declaration of Independence and U.S. Constitution, and former senators and governors. Dr. Martin Luther King Jr. became the first African American honored when his portrait was added in 1974.

Inside the building, the Georgia Capitol Museum is home to a two-headed snake; cotton bales; an exhibit on Georgia gold (of course); mounted bass, deer, alligators, and raccoons; and other fascinating stuff.

. . . *Gone with the Wind* is more than a book and movie

Fiddle-dee-dee, Miss Scarlett, you've turned 70—as old as Aunt Pittypat when you scandalized her Peachtree Street home, mooning over Ashley. No more the belle of the barbecue, you've held up amazingly well since Margaret Mitchell introduced you on the opening pages of *Gone with the Wind* way back in 1936. Just imagine! She was going to call you Pansy O'Hara.

You captivated us with your opening monologue—"War, war, war, this war talk's spoiling all the fun at every party this spring. I get so bored I can scream"—and still had us firmly in your hands 1,037 pages later, when Rhett walked out and you vowed, "Tomorrow is another day," the original title of the book.

The novel won the Pulitzer Prize for fiction, and in the ensuing seven decades, 30 million copies in dozens of languages have been sold (topped only by the Bible). About 250,000 are purchased in the United States every year and 100,000 elsewhere.

The movie, which premiered in 1939, has reputedly been seen by more people, in more countries, than any other film. It has grossed (adjusted for ticket price inflation) nearly $4 billion.

At any given moment, somewhere on earth, first-time readers and returnees are holding their breath as they turn the pages

Gone with the Wind:

Still loved and read and seen on the screen after more than 60 years.

on Miss Scarlett's adventures. Will she ever get her hands on the sainted Ashley? Will she ever be hungry again? Somewhere, the dramatic introduction is unfolding on TV and movie screens. "There was once a land of cavaliers and ladies fair. . . ."

Visitors invariably ask, "Just where is Tara?" Mitchell situated the O'Haras' fictional plantation in Clayton County. What with Atlanta burning and Yankees marauding everywhere, it seems like leagues away from Aunt Pitty's house, but it's actually just south of downtown Atlanta. If it ever did really exist, it would have been buried long ago under the runways of Hartsfield-Jackson International Airport.

you know you're in
georgia when...
...the Girl Scouts' founder's mother is a romantic ghost story

In the 1880s workmen were digging in Savannah's Wright Square for a monument to William Washington Gordon, founder of the Georgia Railroad. They inadvertently unearthed the bones of Tomochichi, the Yamacraw chief who had befriended the city's founder, General James Oglethorpe. They reported their discovery to Eleanor Kinsey Gordon, the daughter-in-law of James Gordon and the mother of Girl Scouts founder Juliette Gordon Low. Let me tell you a story a tour guide once told me.

Mrs. Gordon had forgotten that Tomochichi had been buried in the square after his death in the late 1700s. Embarrassed over the incident, she ordered a large granite stone that was then placed on Tomochichi's reburied bones in Wright Square.

Although she asked many times for a bill, the Stone Mountain Granite Company never replied. After a decade of repeated requests, the company sent a bill for a dollar, "due on Judgment Day." Mrs. Gordon sent a check for a dollar with this curt note: "I'll be much too busy on Judgment Day to pay my debts."

On the day she died, that prophesy apparently was fulfilled. As she lay dying, she called her husband's name. He was William Washington Gordon II, who had died five years before. Most people called him the Old Captain, his Confederate Army rank.

She reputedly grew quiet again, and her daughter-in-law, Margaret, excused herself and walked downstairs to the parlor. As she rested there, a man in the prime of life, dressed in a Confederate officer's uniform, appeared, then acknowledged her without speaking and walked to the front steps. Moments later, Margaret's husband came in and said, "Mother just passed away." Margaret said, "Didn't you see your father?" He told her she'd been dreaming.

When they walked down the front steps of the house, a servant said, "I just saw the Old Captain and he told me, 'It's 4 o'clock, I'm taking Miss Eleanor for her afternoon carriage ride.'"

Just as Eleanor had predicted, she was much too busy on Judgment Day to worry about her debts.

Gordon, Eleanor Kinsey:

This Savannah matriarch is at the heart of a romantic ghost story.

47

you know you're in
georgia when . . .
. . . grits is groceries

Go down the cereal aisle of most any Georgia market, and you'll see grits to the right of you, grits to the left of you. White grits, yellow grits, speckled-heart grits, quick grits. And something called "instant grits," which aren't grits at all but chemical flakes that, when mixed with boiling water, create a noxious porridge some suspect is a plot hatched in New Jersey to undermine a pillar of Southern culinary culture.

The real thing is finely or coarsely ground corn meal, cooked to a creamy consistency and brought to perfection with ample helpings of butter, salt, and pepper or with cheese and a few dashes of Tabasco. It's not Cream of Wheat or oatmeal. Whatever you do, don't add sugar—the grits will combust with shame.

In 2002 the Georgia General Assembly ordained grits as "the official processed food of the State of Georgia." House Bill 993 established nine clauses about grits, among them:

(1) Grits are bits of ground corn or hominy which constitute a uniquely indigenous Southern food first produced by Native Americans many centuries ago; and

(2) Grammatically, the word "grits" enjoys the notable distinction of being a rare noun which is always plural but which may properly be used as either singular or plural in writing and speaking; and

(3) According to the October, 1999, issue of *Smithsonian Magazine*, it can even be argued that grits are America's first food . . . ; and

(4) This prepared food is well known to all Georgians . . . but may initially be a source of confusion to newly arrived visitors, especially those who have been told that they grow on grits trees; and

(7) It has been said of grits with literal truth that no one can eat just one.

Most locals praise the food in simpler terms by simply declaring that "Grits is groceries."

In 2002 lawmakers also declared Warwick, in southwest Georgia's Worth County, the state's grits capital in recognition of its annual National Grits Festival.

Grits:

It's a fact: Grits is groceries.

If ever there was a stalwart son of the South, it was Lewis Grizzard (born October 20, 1946). Reared in tiny Moreland, 40 miles south of Atlanta, he published his first humorous stories, about his Little League team, in the local newspaper. At age 23 he became the youngest sports editor in the history of the *Atlanta Journal*.

Then, in what he recalled as "the most miserable time in my life," Grizzard went north as sports editor of the *Chicago Sun-Times*. He summed up his homesick feelings in an autobiographical book titled *If I Ever Get Back to Georgia, I'm Gonna Nail My Feet to the Ground*.

When he did get back, he "nailed his feet" with a humor column in the Atlanta papers, where his favorite topics—University of Georgia football; his dog, Catfish; his mama; apple-pie patriotism; pickup trucks; barbecue; and the sweet, simple life of fictional and factual folks in Moreland— struck a chord with Georgians, fellow Southerners, and people all over the country.

Grizzard also wrote candidly, and with typical humor, about his three divorces and his struggles with alcoholism and a congenital heart condition. At his peak he was syndicated in 450 newspapers in such seemingly unlikely places as Boston, New York, Chicago, and Los Angeles.

Grizzard, Lewis:

Mark Twain in Gucci loafers.

Grizzard's 23 books include *Kathy Sue Loudermilk, I Love You*; *Don't Bend Over in the Garden, Granny, You Know Them Taters Got Eyes*; and *Elvis Is Dead and I Don't Feel So Good Myself*.

After Grizzard died in 1994 at age 48, some of his ashes were scattered at the 50-yard line at Sanford Stadium, home of his beloved Georgia Bulldogs. The Lewis Grizzard Museum in Moreland exhibits his books, typewriter, Gucci loafers, and other memorabilia.

you know you're in
georgia when...
...you're in Oliver Hardy's hometown

When Oliver Hardy was born in Harlem, Georgia, in 1892, his parents christened him Norvell, an old family name. The name never fit his gregarious personality, so in later years he changed it to Oliver in tribute to his father, a Confederate veteran who had died when Hardy was a youngster.

Small-town Harlem (in east Georgia near Augusta) was also an improper fit, so Hardy moved on and never really looked back. He ran away from home to join a traveling theatrical troupe, and when his mother sent him to Atlanta to study music, he skipped his lessons to sing in a vaudeville house.

While managing a movie theater in Milledgeville in 1910, Hardy reckoned he could out-act the actors on the silent screen. He pursued his ambition with a fledgling studio in Jacksonville, Florida, where he made 50 short one-reelers.

In Los Angeles in the early 1920s, he made his first film with a young British comedian named Stan Laurel. The pair didn't click as a team until the late 1920s, when audiences rolled in the aisles at their antics in such classics as *The Battle of the Century,* which featured one of the biggest pie fights ever filmed.

While "talkies" were the undoing of many silent-movie careers, Laurel and Hardy prospered in the new medium. Their comical mishaps in more than 100 films kept the

Hardy, Oliver:

The beloved comedian took the "A Train" from Harlem and never looked back.

world laughing through the Great Depression and World War II.

The pair worked in radio, on the stage, and in television until Hardy went to cinema heaven in 1957, followed a few years later by Laurel. Beloved by audiences worldwide, they won their only Oscar for *The Music Box,* named the Best Short Film of 1932.

Hardy's hometown keeps their memory alive with a museum and the annual Laurel and Hardy Festival. On the first Saturday of October, thousands of fans join parades, a street dance, and a look-alike contest and enjoy some hearty laughs as Ollie turns another situation to hash, wrings his derby like a chicken's neck, and fumes at Stan, "This is another fine mess you've gotten us into."

you know you're in
georgia when . . .
. . . you land at the world's busiest airport

Eat your heart out, O'Hare, JFK, Heathrow, and Charles de Gaulle. Atlanta's Hartsfield-Jackson International Airport is the world's champion at putting people on airplanes. It achieved that lofty station through the efforts of the two air-minded mayors in its hyphenated name.

William Berry Hartsfield, mayor from 1937 to 1961, was smitten by the aviation bug as a young man, when he was taken aloft by early 1900s barnstormers. As a city alderman he pushed for the city's first paved runways. In the 1930s the Federal Aviation Administration was plotting a southern transcontinental route from Los Angeles to New York and many cities were competing for the honor of being a stopover city. Hartsfield wined and dined the visiting scouts and filled their heads with so much Atlanta blarney that the city, which didn't have a lighted runway, won over rival Birmingham, which did.

The rest is history. Hartsfield built the first jet-age terminal and lived to see "his" airport's first international flights, to Mexico. Nowadays, you can step on a plane in Atlanta and step off in Johannesburg, Moscow, Seoul, or Buenos Aires.

Maynard Holbrook Jackson's name was added in 2004. The city's first African-American mayor, Jackson was elected to the first of three terms in 1973. He was responsible for construction of the current airport complex, one of Georgia's largest private employers. He died in 2003.

Some years before Communist China's capitalistic ascendancy, an airport official taking visiting Chinese officials on a tour proudly remarked, "This is the world's busiest airport." To which a puzzled Beijing dignitary replied, "Is that good?"

As the saying goes, "Whether you're going to heaven or hell, you'll have to change planes in Atlanta."

Hartsfield-Jackson International Airport:

If you've ever flown, you've probably changed planes here.

you know you're in
georgia when...
...you're in North America's most haunted city

Ghosts and rumors of ghosts have haunted Savannah since the first English settlers founded the port city in 1733. So many restless specters roam cemeteries, historic houses, and picturesque squares that para-psychologists say it has the dubious distinction of having North America's highest density of restless deceased. They contend that an electromagnetic charge in the sandy soil makes it difficult for some human spirits to depart.

Whatever the reason, over the centuries reports have circulated of ghostly pirates, Revolutionary and Civil War soldiers, African-American slaves, dueling victims, jilted lovers, Native Americans uprooted from their graves, even cats and dogs still looking for their masters. Long-deceased owners of historic-district restaurants come back to check on their guests.

Numerous books chronicling the city's otherworldly residents have inspired more than two dozen "ghost tours" that give thousands of annual visitors a sometimes-chilling look at the colorful history and quirky personality of Georgia's oldest city. Walking tours have the highest spook factor; you never know when something's going to go "bump" in the azalea bushes.

Jim Williams, the protagonist in John Berendt's nonfiction best seller *Midnight in the Garden of Good and Evil,* figures in one of the city's ongoing ghost stories. While he

Haunted Savannah:

Even your house cat might be a "haint."

was restoring the Hampton Lillibridge House on Saint Julian Street, strange noises and spectral sightings sent workmen fleeing to the street. The psychology department at Duke University found electromagnetic shifts in the 150-year-old house. An Episcopal bishop conducted an exorcism in 1963, to no avail.

Over the years occupants have reported hearing unexplained noises and classical music coming from the walls, seeing objects levitating, and feeling cold spots in several rooms. Williams himself never lived in the house; instead, he purchased the Mercer House on Monterey Square, where he shot and killed his associate, Danny Hansford (the reason for this was unclear). After Williams's death in the Mercer House in 1989, late-night passersby reported seeing lights and hearing the sounds of gala partying from the shuttered mansion.

...hockey thrives in a hot state

Northern "immigrants" have imported "real" bagels, New York cheesecake, Chicago-style pizza, Philly cheese steaks, a passion for the Red Sox and Cubs, and the phrase "you guys" to Georgia.

And hockey. Before the National Hockey League's Atlanta Flames skated into the Omni Arena in the mid-1970s, most Georgians thought ice was something that chilled sweet tea and that you put on your forehead after a night's lollapalooza. A puck was a character in a Shakespeare play.

The Flames weren't very good, but we were just becoming familiar with the Zamboni, blue lines, hat tricks, power plays, high-sticking, icing the puck, slashing, and other features of the game when the team jilted us for Calgary, Alberta, where it still hasn't won the Stanley Cup.

In 1999 Atlanta got a second chance with a new team: the Thrashers, named for the brown thrasher, Georgia's state bird. The team plays on a new rink, Philips Arena, on the site of the Omni, which was worn out after 25 years.

The Thrashers haven't won the Stanley Cup, but in 2005–2006 they missed the NHL playoffs by only two games. The city's Canadians, Northerners, and Southern hockey converts figure it'll happen any year now. After all, the minor-league Gwinnett

Gladiators, who play in the northwest suburbs, went to Alaska to play for the ECHL championship in 2006. All the Glads brought back were sealskin mukluks and freeze-packed salmon, but hope springs eternal, even in the 'burbs.

Columbus and Augusta also put minor-league teams on ice. Sadly, we lost one of the best nicknames in all of professional sports when the Macon Whoopee packed up their pucks and Zamboni and moved to South Carolina.

Hockey:

Flames or Thrashers, they still haven't won the Stanley Cup.

you know you're in
georgia when...
...Doc Holliday is the state's most famous dentist

"Doc Holliday was the most skillful gambler, and the nerviest, fastest, deadliest man with a six-gun I ever saw." Quite a tribute from Wyatt Earp, a pretty tough hombre himself.

John Henry Holliday was born in Griffin, Georgia, on August 14, 1851. His father was a wealthy planter and lawyer who served in the Civil War as a Confederate major. Because of his family's social status, John Henry felt compelled to choose an "honorable" profession. In 1872 he received a Doctor of Dental Surgery degree from the Pennsylvania College of Dental Surgery in Philadelphia. He opened an office in downtown Atlanta but soon came down with tuberculosis, which quashed his practice and sent him west to drier climates.

Holliday first went to Texas, where he learned to drink hard liquor, gamble, and defend himself with a six-gun. He killed a solider in an 1876 gunfight and then moved to notorious Dodge City, Kansas, and Tombstone, Arizona. In Tombstone he teamed up with Wyatt Earp at the legendary gunfight at the O.K. Corral in 1882. Holliday died in Colorado in 1887.

While living in Atlanta, he reputedly courted his first cousin Mattie Holliday, a relative of novelist Margaret Mitchell. According to an exhibit in the Margaret Mitchell House Museum in Atlanta, they parted when Doc went west and Mattie joined a Savannah convent, where she took the name Sister Mary Melanie.

In the 1920s Mattie and Margaret Mitchell became friends, and she gave the author permission to use her convent name, Melanie, for one of her main characters in the now-famous novel. Doc was purportedly the inspiration for Southern gentleman Ashley Wilkes, whom Mitchell married to Melanie in *Gone with the Wind,* although his character is more akin to Rhett Butler's.

Bill Dunn, with the Doc Holliday Society in Griffin, says there's no doubt that Doc and Mattie knew each other, but there's no evidence that they ever intended to marry. Dunn's museum in his home includes one of the only tangible souvenirs of Doc's brief life here, a foundation stone from the Holliday family's plantation house.

Holliday, Doc:

Are you sure you need that six-shooter for a root canal?

you know you're in
georgia when...
...you find yourself in Hollywood South

"Lights, cameras, action!" Could this be Georgia? Sure enough. The state is portrayed in dozens of big-screen and television movies from the highbrow *Driving Miss Daisy* to the lowbrow *Dumb and Dumberer.*

The state often plays itself, as in *Midnight in the Garden of Good and Evil* (Clint Eastwood's adaptation of John Berendt's best seller about Savannah's peccadilloes) and the Oscar-winning *Forrest Gump.* Sometimes it stands in for another locale, as Savannah did when it doubled as antebellum Boston in the Civil War drama *Glory.*

Small towns show up pretty as a picture. Consider *Fried Green Tomatoes,* filmed at the real-life Whistle Stop Cafe in Juliette; *To Dance with the White Dog,* the celluloid version of Royston native Terry Kay's charming best seller, filmed in Plains and Americus; and the *In the Heat of the Night* television series, filmed in Covington.

Georgia emerged as a prime location for the film industry in the 1970s, when favorite son Burt Reynolds, a Waycross native, made a string of cornball-but-popular movies such as *The Longest Yard, Gator, Smokey and the Bandit,* and *Sharkey's Machine* at such diverse locales as the state prison and Atlanta's Peachtree Plaza Hotel. Reynolds also co-starred in 1972's *Deliverance,* which delivered a mixed mes-

Hollywood South:

Georgia is portrayed in dozens of big-screen and television movies, often playing itself.

sage about the state's scenic Blue Ridge Mountains.

The mountains got a more sympathetic treatment in the 1950s, when Susan Hayward portrayed a preacher's wife in *I'd Climb the Highest Mountain.* In 1957 Hayward married Georgian Eaton Chalkey; they raised horses and cattle on his Carroll County ranch, and Hayward was buried there after her death in 1972.

Alas, the most famous movie about the state—*Gone with the Wind*—was shot entirely in Hollywood.

55

...the Honeymooners are together again

More than fifty years after *The Honeymooners* went to the big sitcom in the sky, Ed, Trixie, Ralph, and Alice are back in the swim—in the Georgia Aquarium in downtown Atlanta. This time around, the Nortons (played by Art Carney and Joyce Randolph) and the Kramdens (played by Jackie Gleason and Audrey Meadows) have been reborn as whale sharks.

The biggest fish in the world are the stars in the biggest fish tank in the world. They share the 8-million-gallon aquarium's 6.2-million gallon Ocean Voyage exhibit.

Ralph and Ed took up housekeeping six months before the girls. They made the 8,000-mile journey from Taiwan in time for the aquarium's November 2005 dedication. Fifteen-foot-long juveniles, the gentle, plankton-eating pair flew to Atlanta in the first-class comfort of a specially configured UPS Boeing 747.

The males have taken to Georgia cooking so well that they've gained more than 3 feet and several hundred pounds each. Marine biologists say that they eventually will reach the approximate size of the buses Ralph piloted around New York City.

Alice and Trixie joined the guys in June 2006. If they hadn't been rescued from a fishing boat, they were destined, like the fellows, for Taiwanese dinner tables. The

The Honeymooners:

Together again in the Georgia Aquarium.

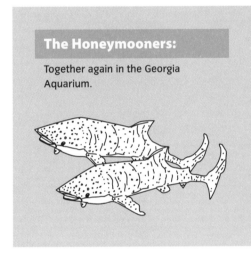

foursome make up the largest whale shark exhibit anywhere in the world. They're classified as sharks, but are called whales (as in whale shark) for their prodigious size.

When they reach full maturity, the quartet will hopefully mate and fill the tank with offspring. But if Mrs. Kramden should take a shine to Ed, aquarium visitors might hear Ralph booming, ". . . to the moon, Alice, to the moon!"

Georgians and other Southerners tradition-ally begin the new year with a glut of col-lege football bowl games and big servings of Hoppin' John, a dish that had a dark beginning spouting from the African-American slave culture, that combines white rice, black-eyed peas, ham hocks, onions, red peppers, chicken stock, and other variables. An old Southern saying contends: "Eat poor that day, eat rich the rest of the year. Rice for riches, and peas for peace."

True-blue traditionalists plant a shiny new dime in the peas, and whoever bites into the coin (hopefully not swallowing it or breaking a tooth) is assured of good luck during the coming year. For maximum good fortune, the first bites should be consumed at the stroke of midnight on New Year's Eve, with toasts of champagne. Eat Hoppin' John with collard greens and cornbread, and you can count your fortune before year's end.

Hoppin' John recipes and preparation vary from cook to cook. Some cook the peas and rice in one pot; others simmer them separately, blending them in the serving dish. Some top off the dish with chopped raw onions and splashes of Tabasco sauce, whereas others add spicy sausage and bacon.

Real Southern cooks would no more use canned black-eyed peas than they would put instant grits on their family's breakfast table. Only dried peas—soaked, rinsed, sorted through for pebbles and grit, and drained dry on paper towels—make an honest Hoppin' John, assuring good taste and good luck. Black-eyed peas don't taste like any other peas because they're really beans.

Why is the dish called Hoppin' John? South Carolinians say it goes back to the early 1840s, when it was sold on the streets of Charleston by a handicapped man known as ... you guessed it. More humorous leg-ends contend that a "man named John came hoppin'" when his wife put the dish on the table.

Hoppin' John:

Eat it on New Year's Eve or New Year's Day for good luck.

you know you're in
georgia when . . .
. . . hushpuppies are for eating, not for wearing

Hush Puppies are casual footwear. *Hushpuppies* are one of the South's favorite side dishes. Hand-shaped dumplings of cornmeal, buttermilk, baking soda, egg, chopped onions, baking powder, salt, pepper, and sugar, they're deep-fried in lard or the same oil as their soul mate, catfish filets. Barbecue often comes with the crunchy little bits; they're perfect for dunking into spicy sauce and Brunswick stew.

The name has a number of possible origins. The oldest dates back to 1720s New Orleans, when French Ursuline nuns hand-shaped cornmeal and other ingredients into a dish they called *croquettes de maise* ("corn croquettes"), which were later called hushpuppies by people who didn't speak French. Easily transported by ships and horseback, the croquettes were very likely North America's first fast take-out food. Pretty soon, hushpuppies were showing up from coast to coast, but especially in the Deep South.

An apocryphal story says that an African-American cook in Georgia was frying a mess of catfish and cornmeal dumplings when dogs in the yard began howling for a handout. To shush their yapping, she tossed them some of her dumplings, exhorting the animals to "Hush, you puppies." The same story is attributed to cooks, hunters, trappers, fishermen, and Civil War soldiers from Louisiana to Virginia.

If you'd like to try your hand at whipping up a batch of these delicacies, mix together two and a half cups of cornmeal, one-half cup of all-purpose flour, two teaspoons of baking powder, one teaspoon of salt, and one teaspoon of sugar. Add one and a half cups of buttermilk or flat beer, two-thirds of a cup of chopped onions, one-half cup of bacon drippings or melted lard, and one beaten egg. Mix together lightly.

The batter should be a little stiff. Drop by heaping teaspoonfuls into hot fat. The hushpuppies should bounce to the surface in about three minutes. Turn them over and brown for an additional two to three minutes. Remove the hushpuppies and drain on paper towels.

Hushpuppies:

Put 'em on the table, and your "puppies" will shush their yapping.

you know you're in
georgia when...
...you're at America's oldest state park

Pee-ew! That water smells like rotten eggs. Probably even the Creek Indians, who were imbibing it centuries before white men came into central Georgia, held their noses at the rank odor. Supposedly it was good for whatever ailed them, though, so no doubt they drank it like kids taking their cod liver oil.

Nowadays, all manner of people come to Indian Springs State Park, near Jackson, in hopes of finding health in the aromatic spring waters.

In 1800, about a decade after the first white settlers came into the area, Creek Chief William McIntosh built a cabin beside the springs. Born in 1775 McIntosh was the son of a British military officer and a Creek woman from a prominent clan. He led the Lower Creek (mainly in Georgia) in an alliance with American forces during the War of 1812. He served under Andrew Jackson against Upper Creek (mainly in Alabama) in 1813–1814 and in the Seminole Wars in Florida in 1817–1818, when he was commissioned a brigadier general in the United States Army.

In 1825 McIntosh and eight other chiefs signed the Treaty of Indian Springs, ceding all Creek land in Georgia to the state for $400,000. Historians contend that Georgia was determined to possess the Creek lands at any cost and that McIntosh signed the treaty to forestall bloodshed.

Indian Springs State Park:

A turbulent past and peaceful present coexist in America's oldest state park.

The Creek didn't see it that way. They denounced McIntosh as a traitor, and he was assassinated three months after he signed the treaty. When the Creek were moved out on the Trail of Tears, the town of Indian Springs was founded. The state acquired land around the spring and opened it to the public in 1825, unofficially making it the nation's first state park. A century later it officially joined the state park system.

The springhouse and other mellow fieldstone buildings were created by the Civilian Conservation Corps during the Great Depression. The Indian Museum displays artifacts and information on the park's history. Around a 105-acre lake, visitors enjoy a swimming beach, fishing, rental boats, nature trails, a picnic area, campsites, and cottages.

It's a good 10,000 miles or so, as the jets fly, from the hills of northeast Georgia to the Outback wilds of central Australia. If you've always wanted to see kangaroos in their natural habitat but can't find the time or the money, the Kangaroo Conservation Center, near Dawsonville, has all the 'roos you could ever want to see. More, in fact, than any other place outside of Australia itself.

Debbie and Roger Nelson brought the first of their hip-hopping marsupials—which now number more than 250—to their 87-acre Dawson County "Outback" in the 1990s. The animals are bred for zoos and animal sanctuaries as far away as China. The kangaroos have a supporting team of other exotic birds and animals from Australia, Africa, and the tropics.

Visitors to the Center can learn how to throw a boomerang, investigate the differences between kangaroos and wallabies, and discover that koalas aren't bears but marsupials that carry their young in pouches, like kangaroos. Perhaps the most fun opportunity is an "earth-friendly" tour in a 10-wheel-drive, open-air army truck. The tour proceeds through a fenced-in sanctuary where "mobs" of kangaroos (as groups of them are called) hop up close and gaze at you with big, soulful eyes, then hop away again to report on the curious creatures riding the "big monster with round feet." Newborn joeys peek from their mamas' pouches.

Kangaroo Conservation Center:

An Outback adventure in the wilds of Dawson County.

The tour includes a visit to a barn. Here visitors may be lucky enough to have a close encounter with kangaroos, which weigh 150 to 200 pounds, and the lovable dik-dik, an endangered miniature East African antelope no bigger than a house cat.

In 2005 the Nelsons opened Aussie Walkabout, a ¼-mile hiking path. In Billabong Encounter, an indoor-outdoor aviary/greenhouse, eucalyptus trees and other Australasian plant and tree species shelter *bettongs*, tiny, endangered brush-tailed kangaroos; Bennett's wallaby and agile wallaby, rarely seen in North America; blue-winged kookaburras; and Australian kingfisher birds, whose loud cry is reminiscent of someone laughing abruptly at a joke.

you know you're in
georgia when ...
... it's still the law in Kennesaw

In 1982 the town of Kennesaw, in northern Cobb County, enacted a law to protect the lives and well-being of its 7,000 citizens. Ordinance 34-1 decreed: "In order to provide for and protect the safety, security and general welfare of the city and its inhabitants, every head of household residing in the city limits is required to maintain a firearm, together with appropriate ammunition. . . ."

Convicted felons, physically and mentally disabled persons, and those who opposed gun ownership on religious or other grounds were exempt from the mandate.

The ink was barely dry when Kennesaw became the talk of the civilized world. The city fathers who sired the legislation showed up on talk shows to explain their pistol-packin' law. Back on the home front, citizens embarrassed by their town's sudden notoriety filed lawsuits challenging the ordinance's legality.

The local constabulary refrained from raiding citizens' domiciles to check for compliance, and, after a short time, the ordinance was amended to exclude those who couldn't afford firearms or objected to them for whatever reason.

Thus, the only people who were subject to the law were those who agreed with it. In the 25 years since Ordinance 34-1 went on the books, Kennesaw has mushroomed into a sizable star in the metro Atlanta galaxy, with a state university campus, a Wal-Mart, a Starbucks, and more than 20,000 citizens, some formerly from New Jersey, Mexico, Southeast Asia, southern California, and other faraway places.

By and large, citizens view the law as a relic of bygone days, like the Civil War locomotive *General,* which is showcased in the town's Smithsonian-affiliated Southern Museum of Civil War and Locomotive History.

Kennesaw Gun Law:

Still a law that's never been enforced.

you know you're in
georgia when . . .
. . . an alien vine can mummify you in a heartbeat

It's Supervine! Faster than a speeding bullet! More powerful than a locomotive! Leaps tall buildings at a single bound! Its real name is kudzu, and it shrouds the shrubbery in suburban backyards and hammerlocks trees from the Blue Ridge Mountains to the Georgia coastal islands.

Slick green leaves the size of dinner plates, with roots tipping the scales at nearly 400 pounds, take over vacant lots, scale fences and utility poles, and bury billboards, barns, abandoned houses, stalled cars, and idle tractors. Stand still too long in one place in spring and summer, when vines can grow a foot a day, and it'll have you in a sleeper hold faster than the Masked Frijole.

Kudzu is part of our landscape, entwined in our folklore. It's the butt of jokes ("How do you plant kudzu? Just drop the seeds and run like a scalded polecat").

By all accounts, credit (blame) goes to the Japanese, who brought kudzu over as an ornamental vine for their pavilion at the 1876 Philadelphia Centennial Exposition. Watching it grow was one of the exposition's big attractions. *Pueraria lobata* (its formal name), a native of the Southeast Asia rain forests, found a happy home in the hot, humid land below the Mason-Dixon Line.

It had so many uses that some called it the "miracle plant." Cattle, hogs, and chickens ate it up. With a chunk of fatback or streak o' lean, kudzu's jade leaves could be boiled for a few hours and served like turnip or collard greens. Dipped in egg batter, it fries up like okra. Home economists developed jams, jellies, soap, and paper from the leaves and herbal medicines from the roots.

As it creeps north of the Mason-Dixon Line, the green monster is acquiring a new handle: "The Confederacy's Revenge." Look out, Gettysburg, here it comes!

Kudzu:

This overachieving vine came as a guest for our 1876 birthday party and didn't have the good manners to go home.

you know you're in
georgia when ...
...the Louvre comes to you

Mona Lisa and Venus de Milo won't be coming. They're busy entertaining tourists following the trail of *The Da Vinci Code*. But when the Paris Louvre comes to Atlanta's High Museum of Art from fall 2006 to fall 2009, other treasured paintings, sculptures, furniture, and decorative pieces from the world's greatest art showcase will cross the Atlantic to wow American art lovers.

The "who's who" roster of Old Masters will include Rembrandt, Rubens, Raphael, Durer, and Velasquez. Most of the nearly 200 pieces have never visited the United States; most of them, in fact, have never left the Louvre's hallowed gallery walls.

Louvre Atlanta grew out of a relationship that High Museum director Michael Shapiro forged with Louvre curator Henri Loyrette, who sent exhibits by Picasso, Monet, Van Gogh, Matisse, and other French artists to the High in the late 1990s and early 2000s.

Even though Mona Lisa won't desert her fans in Paris, the Louvre is sharing several ultra-important paintings. The museum counts *Et in Arcadia Ego,* by 17th-century master Nicolas Poussin, as one of the most important of its 35,000 pieces. Equally revered is Raphael's *Portrait of Baldassare Castiglione.*

The theme of the three-year series is the history and development of the Louvre

Louvre Atlanta:

Mona Lisa is sending several hundred of her closest friends to Atlanta from 2006 to 2009.

from the 17th century, when it was still a royal palace, to the present. Three exhibits scheduled for the first year focus on collections assembled by Kings Louis XIV and the unfortunate Louis XVI, who lost his head during the Revolution.

Louvre Atlanta will be showcased in one of three new wings that Italian architect Renzo Piano designed for the High in 2005.

John Herndon Mercer was born in Savannah in 1909. Before Mercer was a year old he was humming music, and by age 11 he was singing songs he memorized from the radio. He wrote his first lyrics in his early teens.

With no formal musical training, Mercer went to New York in the 1920s, where he sang and wrote lyrics for Paul Whiteman's popular Tin Pan Alley Band. Then it was on to Hollywood, where Mercer got his first big break. Bing Crosby sang his "I'm an Old Cowhand from the Rio Grande" in a 1936 film.

Mercer worked with the composing elite, including Harry Warren, Jerome Kern, Harold Arlen, and Hoagy Carmichael. His songs were featured in *Seven Brides for Seven Brothers, Laura,* Danny Kaye's *Merry Andrew,* and other big hits of the 1940s.

Partnered with Henry Mancini's music, Mercer's lyrics won two Best Song Oscars: one for "Moon River," which Audrey Hepburn crooned in 1961's *Breakfast at Tiffany's* (with the folksy Southern endearment "my huckleberry friend"), and another for the theme music to 1962's *Days of Wine and Roses.*

Mercer won other Oscars for "The Last Time I Saw Paris" in 1942, "On the Atchison, Topeka and the Santa Fe" in 1946, and "In the Cool, Cool, Cool of the Evening" in 1951. Among his numerous other big hits were "Lazybones," "You Must Have Been a Beautiful Baby," "Jeepers Creepers (Where'd You Get Those Peepers)," "That Old Black Magic," "Charade," and "Summer Wind."

Acclaimed the world's greatest lyricist, Mercer died in 1976. A short while later his star was fixed on the Hollywood Walk of Fame. Although he never lived in Savannah again, his old hometown honors him with an exhibit in the Savannah History Museum.

Mercer, Johnny:

This Savannah native wrote the lyrics for "Moon River," "That Old Black Magic," and many other classics.

you know you're in
georgia when...
... Miss Liberty is just down the road a piece

In 1986 the Lions Club of McRae, in southeast Georgia, got so enthused about the 100th anniversary of the Statue of Liberty in New York Harbor that it decided to build a Miss Liberty of its own. Members complemented it with a replica of the Liberty Bell (by giving the old town fire bell a brand-new crack) and an outdoor display of the U.S. Constitution, all "as a reminder to citizens of this great country of what America really means."

The McRae Lions didn't have a lot of cash to finance their patriotic homage, or a lot of statue-building materials. But they had a lot of red, white, and blue spirit. Working with photographs of the original statue as well as scraps and junk they found lying around the town of 2,800, the club built a ½-scale model of Miss Liberty. It's 32 feet tall.

Her head was carved with a chainsaw from a black gum stump pulled out of a Telfair County swamp. Her torch was fashioned out of cypress, and her upraised arm was made from Styrofoam. The hand that holds her torch, illuminated by a working lightbulb, is an oversize electrician's glove into which fresh cement was poured. Sheets sprayed with fiberglass produced her flowing robes.

Miss Liberty:

This McRae lady has a black gum stump for her head and holds aloft a lightbulb beacon.

Dedicated on July 4, 1986, Miss Liberty wasn't intended to be a permanent fixture in downtown McRae's Liberty Square, but townsfolk took a shine to her. Two decades later, she still holds her lightbulb aloft, beckoning the poor, the oppressed, the weary travelers on U.S. Highways 319 and 441.

Julia Roberts, Joanne Woodward, Frances Conroy, Jeff Daniels, and Burt Reynolds were all issued birth certificates somewhere in Georgia.

Academy Award–winner Julia Fiona Roberts, born in Smyrna in 1967, reached megastar status in the early 1990s when she starred opposite Richard Gere in *Pretty Woman*. She later won the Best Actress Oscar and Golden Globe for her critically acclaimed title role in *Erin Brockovich*.

Julia's older brother, Eric Anthony Roberts, had been born in Biloxi, Mississippi, in 1956, but grew up in Smyrna, Georgia. Eric was nominated for a Best Supporting Actor Oscar in 1985 for his role as the escaped Alaska convict Buck in *Runaway Train*.

Born in Thomasville, in southwest Georgia, in 1930, Joanne Gignilliat Trimmier Woodward was influenced by her mother's love of movies. Mom wanted to name her after Joan Crawford, but her parents decided to christen her the more Southern "Joanne" instead. During the 1939 premiere of *Gone with the Wind* in Atlanta, nine-year-old Joanne rushed into the parade of stars and impetuously sat on the lap of a startled Laurence Olivier, who was accompanying his wife, Vivien Leigh, the film's Scarlett O'Hara. Forty years later Woodward starred with Olivier in a television production of *Come Back, Little Sheba*. Woodward won the Best Actress Oscar in 1958 for *The Three Faces of Eve*, about a

Movie Star:

Julia Roberts grew up in the Atlanta suburb of Smyrna.

Georgia woman with multiple personalities. She was nominated for Best Actress for *Rachel, Rachel* (1969); *Summer Wishes, Winter Dreams* (1974); and *Mr. And Mrs. Bridge* (1991), in which her longtime spouse, Paul Newman, co-starred. In 1972 she won Best Actress at the Cannes Film Festival for *The Effect of Gamma Rays on Man-in-the-Moon Marigolds*.

Burton Leon Reynolds Jr. was born in Waycross in 1936. His family moved to Florida when he was young, but several of his nearly 100 films were set in Georgia. They include *Deliverance* (1972), in which Reynolds had his breakout performance, and *Gator* (1976), which he also directed.

Frances Conroy, a Golden Globe and Screen Actors Guild award winner as Ruth Fisher on HBO's *Six Feet Under,* was born in Monroe in 1953. Jeff Daniels, best known for his roles in *Terms of Endearment* (1983), *Dumb and Dumber* (1994), and more recently *The Squid and the Whale* (2005), is an Athens native.

you know you're in
georgia when...
...you're eating a fried Twinkie

Georgians like to deep-fry just about everything—chicken, of course, and dill pickles, cole slaw, hot dogs, okra, corn on the cob, Spam, peach pies, Oreos, etc.

Fried Twinkies are the dessert of choice at Mulligan's, a tavern in Decatur's Oakhurst neighborhood. Owner Chandler Goff and his crew dredge a pair of the sweet snack cakes in beaten egg, roll 'em in Cap'n Crunch cereal, give 'em a good deep-frying, and top 'em with chocolate sauce and bottled cherries. Yu-umm.

The Twinkies are usually the reward for polishing off Mulligan's signature dishes, the Luther Burger and the Hamdog. Late blues singer Luther Vandross was the inspiration for the Luther. The story goes that Vandross woke up hungry one night and craved a hamburger. He didn't have any burger buns, so he improvised by slicing a Krispy Kreme doughnut and putting the grilled hamburger between the halves with slices of cheese.

Goff's edition features a grilled half-pound burger patty topped with cheese and slices of bacon, with a substantial side of fries. The Luther became nationally renowned when *Tonight Show* host Jay Leno read a newspaper story about it and brought Goff to California in June 2005 to prepare it on the show. It was a culinary sensation.

Really big appetites can pair the Luther with the Ultimate Hamdog, a beef hot dog wrapped in a hamburger patty, fried, and served on a hoagie roll with chili, bacon, and a fried egg and french fries on top.

Because Mulligan's has a stake in its patrons' continuing good health, this advice is included on the menu: "We here at Mulligan's hope you have the sense to realize that, although delicious, we do not recommend eating fried foods every day and remind you to exercise regularly and get an annual physical."

Mulligan's:

The Luther, the Ultimate Hamdog, and fried Twinkies take center stage at this Decatur eatery.

One fine day in the 1960s, a four-year-old hunting dog went off in the northwest Georgia woods on an adventure with his owner. He was distracted from his mission by a raccoon or squirrel that took refuge in a hollow chestnut oak tree. Obeying his nose, the dog scurried up the tree in pursuit.

The prey found its way out of the tree, but the poor dog could not. He was wedged in so tightly that he couldn't move, and he ultimately died there. The master apparently never knew what happened to his canine companion.

Instead of decaying, the dog was naturally mummified in his log coffin. His scent went up the well-ventilated tree like it would a chimney, so predators and insects never got wind of him. And resins from the core of the tree helped preserve his corpse.

That would have been the end of the story, but more than 20 years after his demise, loggers cutting trees chopped down the dog's "coffin" and, to their surprise, found the petrified dog still inside.

Rather than send the log to a sawmill, the loggers donated both the log and the encapsulated dog to the Southern Forest World Museum in Waycross, dedicated to informing the public about the importance of the South's forest industry.

Mummified Dog:

A petrified dog is one of the more unusual exhibits at the Southern Forest World Museum in Waycross.

Other exhibits at the museum inclue a logging train, logging tools, and exhibits about Southern forests and tree conservation.

It's ghostly quiet around New Echota these days. A few tourists look at the exhibits and watch the film in the visitor center, then walk the wide streets, past the mostly empty buildings. Courts are not in session, no one's home in the log and plank houses, fields are untilled, and nothing's being poured in Vann's Tavern, which lists room and board for 25 cents, clean sheets for a dime, and whiskey for 12 cents a shot.

In the office of the *Cherokee Phoenix,* visitors are given copies of a newspaper printed in the Cherokee language, which was transcribed into written form by a scholar named Sequoyah in 1821.

What a difference a couple of centuries makes. In 1825 the Cherokee Legislature established New Echota as the capital of a nation that stretched over millions of acres of Alabama, Georgia, Tennessee, and North Carolina. Near modern-day Calhoun, in northwest Georgia, they laid out streets 60 feet wide to accommodate wagons and teams of horses.

The Cherokees' governmental system was modeled on that of the United States, with a written constitution, elected leaders, and a supreme court and other offices that convened in public buildings around a two-acre square.

Most of the Cherokee were farmers who grew corn, beans, and other crops, some

with the labor of black slaves. They kept up with the news through the bilingual *Cherokee Phoenix,* which was published from 1828 to 1834. The last editions chronicled the end of the Cherokee Nation.

When gold was discovered on Cherokee land in the late 1820s, white settlers rushed in. The state of Georgia, supported by President Andrew Jackson, confiscated all Cherokee territory, and in the late 1830s it forced the Indians into exile west of the Mississippi. Thousands perished on this Trail of Tears.

Destroyed after the Cherokee departed, New Echota has been reconstructed as a state historic site. Listen closely and you might hear ghostly voices in the winds blowing through the empty capital.

New Echota:

Ghosts of a proud people haunt their Georgia capital.

you know you're in
georgia when...
...you're in the home of two Nobel Peace Prize winners

Any state would be proud of having one homegrown Nobel Peace Prize winner. Georgia is doubly proud to claim two. Dr. Martin Luther King Jr. won in 1964 for "exceptional advancement of the principles of human liberty." Jimmy Carter won in 2002 "for his efforts to find peaceful solutions to international conflicts, to advance democracy and human rights and to promote economic and social development."

King was born in downtown Atlanta's "Sweet Auburn" neighborhood on January 15, 1929. He enrolled at Atlanta's Morehouse College at age 15. In 1954 he became pastor of Dexter Avenue Baptist Church in Montgomery, Alabama, where he directed the Montgomery bus boycott.

In August 1963 King delivered his dynamic "I Have a Dream" speech at Washington's Lincoln Memorial. In April 1968, while supporting striking sanitation workers in Memphis, Tennessee, he delivered his final address, in which he said, "I've been to the mountaintop . . . I'm not fearing any man." King was assassinated the following day on the balcony of the Lorraine Motel, now the centerpiece of the National Civil Rights Museum.

In Atlanta, the Martin Luther King Jr. National Historic Site includes his boyhood home, his tomb, Ebenezer Baptist Church, and a National Park Service Visitor Center.

Raised on a southwest Georgia farm, Jimmy Carter was elected the 39th U.S. president in 1976. Highlights of his one-term presidency included the Camp David Accords peace treaty between Egypt and Israel and the treaty that ceded control of the Panama Canal to Panama. Since leaving the presidency, Carter has won worldwide respect for helping resolve international conflicts and numerous other human rights and charitable causes, including cofounding Habitat for Humanity in 1976.

Nobel Peace Prize Winners:

Martin Luther King Jr. and Jimmy Carter have done Georgia doubly proud.

...Flannery O'Connor is the most famous Georgia writer you've probably never read

When she was five years old, Mary Flannery O'Connor got her first 15 minutes of fame. Little Flannery was featured in a movie theater newsreel with the pet chicken she had taught to walk backwards.

"That was the most exciting thing that ever happened to me," she said much later, with her tongue planted firmly in her cheek. "It's all been downhill from there."

She described herself as a "pigeon-toed only child with a receding chin and a you-leave-me-alone-or-I'll-bite-you complex." More than 40 years after her death in 1964, O'Connor is widely viewed as a worthy Southern gothic successor to William Faulkner.

Born in Savannah in 1925, she moved to Milledgeville with her family when she was 13 and spent most of her life there. She majored in English and sociology at Milledgeville's Georgia State College for Women. Her rare forays outside Georgia included the prestigious University of Iowa Writers' Workshop in 1946.

In 1951 O'Connor was diagnosed with disseminated lupus, the same immune system disease that killed her father when she was 15. She sequestered herself at her Milledgeville farm, Andalusia, where she raised peacocks, ducks, chickens, and geese and wrote her two novels—*Wise Blood* (1952) and *The Violent Bear It Away* (1960)—and collections of short stories.

O'Connor, Flannery:

One of Georgia's most famous authors, known only to a select few.

O'Connor drew most of her Southern characters and plotlines from people and situations she observed around her. It was a popular sport among her neighbors to try to discern who among them was strange enough to be the model for Hazel Motes, Francis Marion Tarwater, Rayber, and the other rascals, revivalists, and patient sufferers O'Connor brought to life.

"My characters aren't grotesque," she answered her critics. "It's just the way Southern people are."

She never lost her sense of humor. When an aspiring novelist asked O'Connor if she thought journalism schools discouraged creativity, she replied tartly, "Not nearly enough. No telling how many best-sellers could be prevented by more diligent teachers."

Way back in the 1950s, Hollywood riveted us to our movie seats with a raft of films about the effects of atomic radiation on our bodies and things around us. Caught in an atomic cloud, the Incredible Shrinking Man withered away to a dust mite. Radiation had the opposite effect on other thyroids, like those of the ants in *Them* and the title character in *Attack of the 50 Foot Woman*. And who could eat a salad again after *Attack of the Killer Tomatoes*?

The same must have happened to some innocent plants and creatures here in Georgia. Alongside Interstate 75, near Ashburn, the World's Largest Peanut stands 20 feet high. Down in Plains, a goober with Jimmy Carter's toothy smile is a scary 13 feet tall. At Cornelia, in northeast Georgia, the Big Red Apple is 7 feet high and 22 feet in circumference and weighs in at 5,200 pounds.

The Peach State may not grow the most peaches anymore, but we've surely got one of the largest of the species. Perched on a pedestal on Interstate 75 in the Peach County town of Byron, the Big Peach measures 75 feet from leafy stem to pointy tip and a curvaceous 28 feet at the waist.

A 20-foot Big Rabbit says "What's up, Doc?" in front of the Rabbittown Cafe in Rabbittown.

But Marietta's Big Chicken is the state's most famous mutant. For more than 45

Oddities of Nature:

Art is in the eye of the beholder.

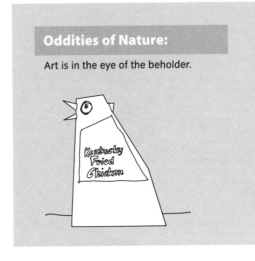

years, motorists navigating Cobb County's maze of highways have set their directional signals on a 56-foot, red-and-white sheet metal rooster that stands watch on the facade of a KFC outlet on U.S. Highway 41/North Cobb Parkway.

KFC reluctantly inherited the Big Chicken when it purchased a Marietta diner in the 1960s. When the big guy was severely injured by a tornado in 1993, public sentiment persuaded KFC's suits to bring it back to life.

As certain as summer drifts into fall and mountain foliage begins its seasonal turn, the sounds of yodeling, accordions, alpenhorns, polkas, and the Chicken Dance and the aromas of bratwurst, sauerkraut, and beer echo through Helen.

Since the 1970s, when the former White County logging town was brought back to life as a faux-Bavarian village with red-tile roofs, geranium boxes, and beer gardens, Oktoberfest has been an integral part of the make-believe *gemütlichkeit*.

From mid-September to early November, the Festhalle overflows with merrymakers in jeans and shorts and lederhosen and dirndls (purchased from shops on Helen's Hauptstrasse/Main Street). The revelers down brats and knacks and steins of German beer as they cavort to the irresistible sounds of the Sauerkrauts, Al Nowak & the Edelweiss Orchestra, Prost, Lorelei and Schatzi, and other "oompah" bands imported from Ohio, Wisconsin, and Pennsylvania.

Like Helen itself, Oktoberfest began modestly, with a couple of bands and a few hundred participants. But just as Helen has grown into one of the state's biggest attractions, Oktoberfest has grown into one of the Southeast's biggest fall parties. About 100,000 people make the yearly pilgrimage to Bavaria in the Blue Ridge.

When they need a break from the festivities, visitors can glut themselves on the wares in Helen's three blocks of shops, which put out Christmas fixings year-round, as well as Tyrolean hats, cuckoo clocks, chocolate truffles, Swiss and Austrian cheeses, strudel and Black Forest cake, and Georgia-made keepsakes and kitsch.

Visitors also can clop through town in horse-drawn carriages, tour the mountain museum's bear and reptile exhibits, pan for gold, go horseback riding, and take a hot-air-balloon adventure.

It's never long before the wheezy sounds of the accordions, the Lorelei voices of the yodelers, and the "oom-pah-pah" of tubas and trumpets send them back to the Festhalle for another clucking, arm-flapping Chicken Dance.

Oktoberfest:

May I have this Chicken Dance?

you know you're in
georgia when...
...old jails never die

In LaGrange, Ashburn, and Greensboro, townsfolk have turned their draconian prisons into museums.

In its first life, in 1892, the Chattahoochee Valley Art Museum, on Lafayette Square in downtown LaGrange, was the formidable Victorian headquarters of Troup County law enforcement. When the sheriff and the jail moved to more modern quarters in the 1970s, the Chattahoochee Valley Art Association saved the nearly century-old landmark from destruction and redid it as its showcase museum. Dreary cell blocks are now four galleries brightened with paintings, sculpture, and other media by local and regional artists and traveling national exhibitions and educational and outreach programs.

The Old Gaol in Greensboro and the former Turner County Jail in Ashburn present a far truer picture of life behind 19th- and early-20th-century bars. Serving as the Greene County hoosegow from 1807 to 1895, the Old Gaol's fortresslike granite walls (2 feet thick), crenellated roofline, and small barred windows were a warning to citizens to resist temptation and stick to the straight and narrow. Those who fell by the wayside were imprisoned in a cold, dark medieval fortress some said was modeled after the notorious Paris Bastille. A noose around the neck and a drop through a second-floor trapdoor were the ultimate wages of sin.

When the Turner County Jail was built in 1906, its florid Romanesque architecture was such a contrast to most every other structure in Ashburn that inmates and law-abiders called it Castle Turner. Jailers and their families kept the grounds so meticulously green and trimmed that travelers sometimes tried to check in for the night.

Those who stop at the Crime & Punishment Museum in the former Turner County Jail can tour the grim, gray cell blocks, the death cell, the hanging hook, and the trapdoor, through which a pair of felons could be sent to eternity in tandem.

After the tour visitors can enjoy a to-die-for Southern–style meal at the Last Meal Cafe, in the jailers' former living quarters.

Old Prisons:

In Georgia, old jails have found new lives as museums.

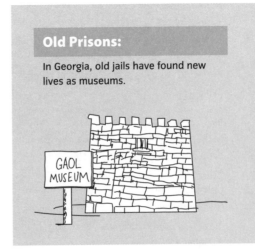

you know you're in
georgia when...
...you enter the world's biggest road race

Georgia celebrates July 4 like every other place in America. Fireworks boom; red, white, and blue parades march through city streets and small-town squares; and people consume tons of ice-cold watermelon, cook hot dogs and burgers on the grill, chase greased pigs, and strut to Sousa marches. In Atlanta, 55,000 people get up at dawn and run down Peachtree Street in pursuit of a T-shirt.

The Peachtree Road Race was the brainchild of members of the Atlanta Track Club, who spent a late-1960s Independence Day running around with infantrymen at Fort Benning in Columbus. On the way home, they thought a race down Atlanta's most famous street would be a dandy way for the city to celebrate the 4th.

When the Peachtree Road Race kicked off in 1970, nobody in his wildest dreams would have imagined it would grow into the largest, best-organized, and most famous 10K (6.2-mile) running event in the world. In an era when those who ran for exercise were viewed as "hippies" or amusing eccentrics, the field that year was a chummy 110. Winners got cheesy trophies, and every finisher was given 25-cent bus fare back to the starting point.

The next year, 198 answered the starting gun, and logo T-shirts were given to all who finished—a prize still coveted today. Run-

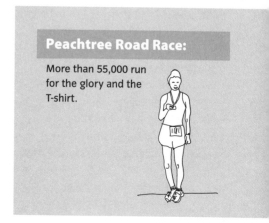

Peachtree Road Race:

More than 55,000 run for the glory and the T-shirt.

ning for exercise was starting on a roll across America; 765 entrants finished the race in 1974, 2,300 in 1975. In the 1980s the field was limited to the first 25,000 to register. Buoyed by Atlanta's bid for the 1996 summer Olympics, the silver anniversary 1995 race was limited to the first 45,000 registrants. The field topped out at 55,000 in the late 1990s.

A celebration of the national holiday and Atlanta's salute to itself, the Peachtree lures the fit, who run religiously every day, as well as nonfit couch potatoes, who do it on a lark or a dare and frequently finish the race in the first-aid tent. The latter sometimes wave the flag and paint their bodies red, white, and blue. Some walk the whole way, just to say they did it.

Every other Atlanta street seems to be called Peachtree Something or Other. Peachtree Street, the main thoroughfare made famous in *Gone with the Wind*, should not be confused—but invariably is—with Peachtree Road, Peachtree Circle, Peachtree Place, Peachtree Lane, Peachtree Parkway, Peachtree Corners Boulevard, Peachtree Corners Circle, West Peachtree Street, Peachtree-Dunwoody Road, Old Peachtree, New Peachtree, Peachtree Drive, Peachtree Industrial Boulevard, Peachtree Battle Avenue, and dozens of other copycats all over the metro area.

When the city's most famous architect wanted a more recognizable address for his new downtown office and hotel complex, he successfully petitioned the Atlanta City Council to change Ivy Street, named for an early pioneer, to Peachtree Center Avenue. The street actually should have been called Pitchtree, for Standing Pitchtree, the name of a Cherokee village that once stood in the heart of what is now downtown. The only real peach trees on Peachtree withered and died when the Macy's department store that maintained them in sidewalk boxes closed a while back.

Gone with the Wind author Margaret Mitchell grew up in a Peachtree Street mansion, demolished decades ago for an office

Peachtree Street:

Miss Margaret and Miss Scarlett made it famous.

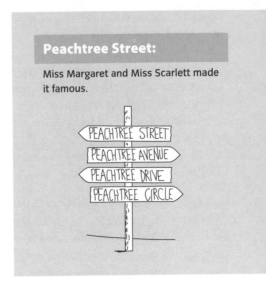

building. When she married she lived in a humbler Peachtree boardinghouse, where she answered her husband's suggestion to "write a book" by tapping out *GWTW* in a basement apartment.

Mitchell made Peachtree famous from Alabama to Afghanistan and, alas, without publishing another word, she perished on it. In 1949, when she was 48, she was hit by a drunk taxi driver while she was crossing the street. She's buried in historic Oakland Cemetery, a few stone's-throws from her beloved thoroughfare.

Georgia could nickname itself the Nutty State, for when it comes to growing peanuts and pecans, we lead the nation. About 40 percent of these two crops come from Georgia. If you've ever bought a jar of peanut butter or baked a pecan pie, chances are you can thank a southwest Georgia farmer.

Jimmy Carter's presidency put the world spotlight on Georgia's "goobers," a nickname thought to be derived from *nguba,* an African word for peanut. About two billion pounds are grown in Georgia every year. There are about 200 peanut pods to the pound and usually two peanuts per pod. This adds up to some 800 billion peanuts. End to end, all those peanuts would extend around the world six million times.

When it comes to pecans, Georgia is most renowned for the "papershell" variety, which requires only slight pressure to crack and yield its tasty meat. In the heart of the pecan belt, around Albany, the state's orchards range in size from a few symmetrical rows of trees to thousands of trees on several thousand acres. All told, more than 145,000 acres produce more than 70 million annual pounds of pecans; skilled cooks turn the crop into enough pecan pies and other treats to join peanuts in their multiple circuits of the globe.

Georgia is third nationally in its third *P* crop: peaches. But real peach appreciators pass on peaches grown in other states and choose the Elberta variety, which Samuel Rumph of Peach County developed in the early 1900s and named for his wife.

Peanuts, Pecans, and Peaches:

We're number one!

Interstate 285, known locally as the Perimeter, is metro Atlanta's equivalent of Washington, D.C.'s Beltway. Around and around it goes for 62.7 miles, a lopsided balloon connecting the suburbs with the inner city and branching off to Interstates 85, 75, 20, 575, and 675 and the Georgia 400 toll road. Some truck drivers call it the Watermelon 500.

Confusing, yes. But you can't get completely lost on it. Keep going around and sooner or later you'll get to where you originally set out for. In 1982 Atlanta Braves pitcher Pascual Perez missed his starting assignment on the mound when he circled the Perimeter twice, looking for Atlanta-Fulton County Stadium. When he finally found his exit and got to the stadium, the game was almost over. He was thereafter nicknamed 285.

The Perimeter opened in 1969, four lanes wide. That was fine, as the metro area had only about 1.5 million residents at the time. But over the years, as the populace has ballooned to 4.7 million, the lanes have grown to 8 and 10 wide. At most times of the day, they are hopelessly gridlocked by the sheer volume of traffic, even when nothing untoward, such as an overturned 18-wheeler, throws in an additional monkey wrench.

The interstate originally cost $90 million, but widening, modernization, and the construction of loop-the-loop interchanges (such as "Spaghetti Junction") have cost close to $400 million. It's the only U.S. freeway with an airport runway overpass. Jets on Hartsfield-Jackson International Airport's fifth runway taxi directly over between I–85 and I–75.

Savvy drivers know to avoid the Perimeter at all times, but especially between 6:00 and 10:00 A.M. and 3:00 and 7:00 P.M. Pity the poor first-timers, because "north" on the highway signs is not really north, east is not east, west is not west, and south is not really south. Only anonymous engineers know how those directions originated, but you do not want to be in the wrong lane at the wrong time.

The Perimeter:

Like the lyrics of the Kingston Trio's "MTA," you can ride forever on I–285 around Atlanta.

you know you're in
georgia when . . .
. . . you "go Pogo"

The Okefenokee Swamp existed for eons before Congress created the Okefenokee National Wildlife Refuge in 1936. But it was a politically savvy 'possum named Pogo who put the half-million-acre swamp, deep in southeast Georgia, on the map.

Pogo was the creation of Walt Kelly, a Connecticut Yankee who introduced the lovable comic strip character in a New York newspaper in 1950. In his early years he was an innocent 'possum, hanging out in the Okefenokee with his pals Albert Alligator, Howland Owl, turtle Churchy-la-Femme, skunk Mam'selle Hepzibah, hound dog Beauregard, seasick duck Mallard de Mer, Deacon Muskrat, and Porky Pine.

By the late 1950s *Pogo* was published in about 600 newspapers and wielded influence far beyond the comic pages. Kelly had strong political opinions, and through Pogo and company he was merciless to those he called Bugbears. Senator Joseph McCarthy, the ruthless Communist "witch-hunter," was lampooned as narrow-minded bobcat Simple J. Malarkey. By holding McCarthy up to ridicule, Pogo helped bring the pompous senator down. He also shot well-aimed arrows, right and left, at Richard Nixon, Spiro Agnew, Fidel Castro, Nikita Khrushchev, George Wallace, and J. Edgar Hoover.

Pogo spoke a blend of Elizabethan English, French, and black and white Southern. In a

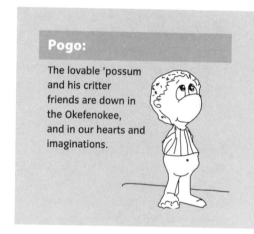

Pogo:

The lovable 'possum and his critter friends are down in the Okefenokee, and in our hearts and imaginations.

poster for Earth Day 1970, he made his most famous observation: "We have met the enemy and he is us."

"I Go Pogo" was a rallying cry for those disenchanted with the political process. Pogo's fellow critters were also witty and wise, as when Porky Pine advised the stressed-out Albert Alligator, "Don't take life so serious, son, it ain't no-how permanent."

Unhappily, in 1973, when 60-year-old Kelly went to the big comic pages in the sky, he took his comic strip with him.

Never fear; Pogo and his friends live on in a series of books. The critters also come out of the swamp during the annual Pogofest at Waycross, the Okefenokee's bright lights, big city.

you know you're in
georgia when...
...you're hiking the Little Grand Canyon

Why go all the way to northern Arizona when you can travel down to southwest Georgia? If you squint with one eye, you can kinda sorta maybe just about imagine that Providence Canyon is like that big tourist draw out west.

Like the Grand Canyon, Providence Canyon—the centerpiece of 1,100-acre Providence Canyon State Park—is a geological layer cake, with bands of rock and soil in subtle shades of purple, tan, salmon, orange, and chalky white. Empower your imagination again, and you can visualize people, bears, rabbits, birds, gnomes, flowers, and other shapes in the formations standing alone in the 16 interlocking canyons.

That Arizona canyon was carved over millions of years by the actions of the Colorado River, which runs turbulently through it. By comparison, Providence Canyon is the geological equivalent of instant grits. In the early 1800s the canyons that make it up were flat, featureless piney woods. Along came settlers, who cleared forests to till corn, sweet potatoes, and other crops. As the trees fell, the roots holding the sand and red clay soil eroded and washed away. With little vegetation as a stopper, rainwater gushed though the exposed terrain, tearing away big chunks.

By the 1850s farmers and their livestock were bogging down in ditches 3 to 5 feet

Providence Canyon:

The maze of canyons was created by nearly two centuries of erosion.

deep. After the Civil War, the pace quickened. Poor cultivation methods went unchecked, and the ditches grew into fair-size gorges, now measuring 150 feet from rim to bottom, ½ mile long, and 300 feet across—and still growing a few inches every year or so.

At the state park the slide show and interpretive exhibits at the visitor center provide an overview before you walk the rim and hike to the canyon's floor. Backpackers overnighting on the backcountry trail are treated to dazzling light shows as sunrise and sunset play on the canyon's walls. Spring and fall embellish the canyon with bouquets of colorful wildflowers.

If you still insist on seeing the "Grand" Canyon, take a left and keep going 1,500 miles or so. You can't miss it.

you know you're in
georgia when . . .
. . . bear and raccoon are on the dinner table

So many bears and raccoons are showing up in the suburbs these days that these exotic Okefenokee Swamp dishes might come in handy someday. They are from-scratch cuisine. The main ingredients, not sold at the supermarket, are an acquired taste (no resemblance to chicken here). Raccoon is dark meat. The fat is strongly flavored and most cooks remove it. The raccoon is usually parboiled before roasting.

Roasted Raccoon: Use one cleaned raccoon carcass, minus the head and paws. Leave ¼-inch of fat on the raccoon. Cover the carcass with a clean cloth moistened with fat. Place on a roasting rack in a shallow pan. Do not cover pan or add water. Bake at 275–300 degrees for three to four hours. Baste several times with drippings, and dust with flour after each basting for a crisp, crackly crust.

Fricasseed Raccoon: Use one raccoon, cut into serving pieces. Remove the fat from the lean meat. Combine ½ cup flour, 1 teaspoon salt, and ½ teaspoon pepper in a bag. Add meat, and shake the bag to coat. Fry the meat in three tablespoons hot fat until brown. Add two cups water, cover, and simmer two hours or until tender. Raccoon goes well with sweet potatoes, collard greens, cornbread or biscuits, and sweet tea.

Bear Meatloaf: Mix one pound ground bear meat, one cup dry breadcrumbs, one package spaghetti sauce mix, ¾ cup water, two beaten eggs, one teaspoon salt, and ½ teaspoon black pepper in a loaf pan. Bake in 375-degree oven for 50 to 60 minutes, or until done.

Note: Please do not try these recipes at home.

Raccoon and Bear Recipes:

One man's meat is another man's. . . .

you know you're in
georgia when...
...you're at the Redneck Games

You can bet your life savings that athletes at the 2008 Summer Olympics in China will not compete in the Hubcap Hurl, the Mud Pit Belly Flop, Bobbing for Pigs' Feet, the Dumpster Dive, Horseshoes with Toilet Seats, or the Armpit Serenade.

Those and other colorful events are featured only at the annual Redneck Games, staged every July at Buckeye Park in East Dublin.

The Games were the inspiration of radio station WQZY, as an in-your-face to the 1996 Summer Olympics three hours north in Atlanta. The Chamber of Commerce and other proper folks around Dublin and East Dublin didn't immediately take to the Games, which they deemed demeaning. Only about 500 showed up for the inaugural Games, but media from as far away as England and Australia have hyped the event's attendance to more than 20,000 in recent years.

The Opening Ceremonies are highlighted by a local character in bib overalls carrying a propane torch adorned with beer can aluminum, leading the athletes into the arena (field) and lighting the "Ceremonial BBQ Grill."

The most eye-catching event is the Mud-Pit Belly Flop, where contestants plunge belly-first into a pool of gooey red Georgia clay mud. The bigger the belly, the bigger the flop and the better your chances of capturing the Gold Medal trophy, with a crushed beer can on top.

Bobbing for Pigs' Feet is another headliner. Similar to kids' bobbing for apples on Halloween, this variation involves thrusting one's head into a bucket of raw swine trotters and coming out with the biggest haul. In 2006 Ashley Richardson, a 19-year-old from Milledgeville, won the competition for the third year running, setting a world record of seven (pigs') feet in 19 seconds.

So what is a Redneck? "A Redneck," one contestant explains, "is somebody who doesn't get a lot of recognition. We love our families and our country and do all the dirty jobs nobody else wants to do. We work hard, we play hard, have fun, and die broke."

Redneck Games:

A belly-flopping, hubcap-tossing, pigs'-feet-surfing good-ol' time.

you know you're in
georgia when...
...you see Rock City

Rock City Gardens is promoted as being near Chattanooga, Tennessee. In fact, the South's most famous attraction is on a wing of Lookout Mountain inside Dade County, Georgia. Tiny Dade (population 13,150) doesn't have a tourism promotion office, so Chattanooga does the promoting and Dade collects Rock City's taxes.

In 1932 Garnet Carter, the founder of Rock City, contributed to popular culture by inventing miniature golf. It seems that a winter guest at Carter's Fairyland Inn wanted to play golf, but the course was closed. So Carter obligingly got together scraps of pipe, carpet, and other materials and built the first putt-putt course in America. It was such a big hit that he franchised it across the country.

That would have been creativity enough for most folks, but Carter and his wife, Frieda, decided to do something with their 10 acres on top of Lookout Mountain, which was studded with all manner of strangely shaped rock formations. The problem was that what they called Rock City was well off the beaten path.

The Carters had an inspiration to paint SEE ROCK CITY on barn roofs all across the eastern United States. Farmers got a few dollars and a new paint job, and Rock City reaped a bonanza of inexpensive publicity. At one time more than 900 barns from Texas to New England urged travelers to come on

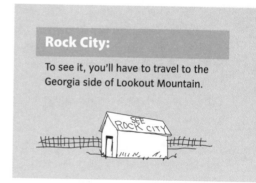

Rock City:

To see it, you'll have to travel to the Georgia side of Lookout Mountain.

down and see what the fuss was all about. The campaign was abetted by red-and-black birdhouses bearing the same invitation.

Seventy-five years later, visitors come from all over the United States and from many foreign countries to visit the Seven States Flag Court, work their way through the Fat Man's Squeeze, take the wobbly Swinging Bridge above a yawning chasm, and peer through the Needle's Eye— just a few of the rock formations at the site. They also can pass through grottoes, glens, and waterfalls and admire the year-round displays of flowering plants.

Even children who've grown up with SpongeBob SquarePants and other contemporary cartoon characters are intrigued by the figures that glow in the ultraviolet light of Fairyland Caverns, also part of the Rock City site. They include Snow White and the Seven Dwarfs, Humpty-Dumpty, and Jack (of the Beanstalk fame).

you know you're in
georgia when...
...you're at Rocktoberfest

While Alpine Helen is entertaining visitors at its Oktoberfest, Rock City Gardens is throwing its annual Rocktoberfest—another celebration of all things German. The latter takes place on weekends in October on the Georgia side of Lookout Mountain.

Helen's German roots go back only about three decades, but Rock City's date to the 1930s, when developer Garnet Carter and his German-born wife, Frieda Utermoeller, opened their gardens and fantastic rock formations to the public.

Frieda marked a trail that wound around the rocks to an outcropping that Native Americans called Lover's Leap. (According to legend, a once-upon-a-time Creek princess threw herself off the precipice when her romance with a warrior from another tribe was thwarted.) Frieda collected wildflowers and other plants and transplanted them along the trail, augmenting them with statues of gnomes and fairy-tale characters imported from her ancestral homeland.

During Rocktoberfest, the roof of the Rock City Pavilion trembles with the Old World sounds of the Sauerkraut Band, the Wurst-

Rocktoberfest:

"Prost!" at Rock City Gardens.

brats, Liederkrantz, and others. Along the *Buddenstrasse* (or Street of Booths) visitors can sample an array of wursts, take Beer 101 classes, and deck themselves out in lederhosen, dirndls, and Tyrolean hats.

you know you're in
georgia when ...
... the Runaway Bride is a bobblehead doll

There once was a would-be bride named Jennifer Wilbanks, who in April 2005 took a very long bus ride. While family and friends and her distraught fiancé looked high and low, "the bride that couldn't" was in far-away New Mexico. When she returned to Duluth, confused and contrite, she 'fessed up to her crime and paid a fine—but, alas, like Humpty-Dumpty, her broken engagement couldn't be put together again.

A year after she returned, the Gwinnett Gladiators, a minor-league hockey team in Wilbanks's hometown of Duluth, commemorated her place in history by giving "Runaway Bride" bobblehead dolls to the first 1,000 attendees at a Sunday game. Fans lined up for three hours, and the bobbleheads—dressed in a bridal veil, sweatshirt, and running shoes—disappeared as quickly as the namesake herself, many turning up overnight on eBay.

"Any similarity to actual persons is unintended and purely coincidental," the Gwinnett Gladiators vowed in a straight-faced statement. To make certain there's no mistaken identity, the base reads "World-Famous Runaway Bride."

The bride made temporary amends with her jilted fiancé. But at last word, she was off on another sad journey, this time to Destination Splitsville.

The Runaway Bride:

Jennifer Wilbanks could run, but she couldn't hide for long.

you know you're in
georgia when...
...the S.S. *Savannah* was the *Spirit of St. Louis* of its day

Was it the dream ship of the future or a steam-powered coffin? Skeptics believed that Davy Jones's locker was the final destination for the steamship *Savannah*. But the spiffy little ship defied its critics when it became the first steam-powered vessel to successfully cross and recross the Atlantic, returning without a single engine bolt or screw out of place.

Financed by wealthy Savannah shipping interests and built in New Jersey shipyards, the *Savannah* made its trial voyage from New York to its namesake port in April 1819. There, President James Monroe and Secretary of War John C. Calhoun came aboard for an inspection cruise of the city's defenses on the Savannah River.

On May 22, 1819, the *Savannah* put to sea on a historic voyage that took her to Liverpool, England, in 29 days and 4 hours, considerably cutting the time of conventional sailing ships. The steam engines performed flawlessly. After receptions by British military officials and members of the royal family, the *Savannah* continued its grand tour with visits to the royal families of Sweden, Norway, Denmark, and Russia.

On November 30 she anchored once again, to wildly cheering crowds, in her home port. But while the mission was technically successful, it was a financial failure. Travelers and shippers were reluctant to trust themselves and their cargo to what many still held was a steam-powered coffin. Nearly three decades would pass before the public would put its faith in steam-powered ocean vessels.

Stripped of her steam-related machinery, the *Savannah* was sold and, ironically, became a success as a conventional cargo carrier. Her life ended tragically in 1823 when she ran aground in a storm off Long Island, New York, and was scuttled.

On May 22, 1944, the U.S. Post Office issued a three-cent stamp commemorating the 125th anniversary of the "First Steamship to Cross the Atlantic." The stamp came out 17 years after Charles Lindbergh's *Spirit of St. Louis* was the first aircraft to make the nonstop crossing.

S.S. *Savannah:*

Her maiden voyage was a precursor of steamships of the future.

86

you know you're in
georgia when...
...you step where General Sherman slept

Marching his Union troops through Georgia in the cold winter of 1864, General William T. Sherman usually shared the cold, cold ground with his men. But in Milledgeville and Savannah rank had its privileges, and the general opted for the very best accommodations the captured towns had to offer.

Milledgeville, in central Georgia, 85 miles southeast of Atlanta, was laid out as the state capital in the early 1800s. By the time Sherman and his 30,000 troops arrived, it was an elegant town where the governor lived in stately luxury in the Palladian-style executive mansion.

Sherman slept in the governor's bedroom, but not in his bed; Governor Joseph E. Brown had taken his bedroom suite with him when he hotfooted it out of town just ahead of the Federals. Sherman was happy to have a roof over his head, and the locals mostly behaved themselves. Except for the state prison, the arsenal, the state archives which were all burned, and molasses poured down the pipes of the Episcopal church, where he stabled his horses, he left Milledgeville pretty much as he found it.

Savannah thoughtfully surrendered without a shot, and Sherman bunked in the early 1850s Gothic Revival Green-Meldrim House on Madison Square. Wealthy merchant Charles Green tactfully left all the furnishings at the general's disposal, and Sherman

Sherman, General William:

Only the best accommodations for good ol' Billy T.

responded by leaving his horses outside and only a few boot scrapes and tobacco juice stains on the chairs and settees.

Guides at what is now St. John's Church parish house point out Sherman's bedroom, now called the Pink Room. Here modern-day bridesmaids primp for the weddings held downstairs in the parlors where Sherman composed a December 22 telegram to his commander-in-chief: "Dear Sir, President Lincoln: I beg to present to you as a Christmas gift, the city of Savannah with 150 heavy guns and plenty of ammunition and about 25,000 bales of cotton."

In the 1980s another William Tecumseh Sherman, a descendant, married a Savannah girl in those very rooms.

you know you're in
georgia when...
...everything's official

Every state has an official flag, official bird, official song, official whatever. When the ladies and gentlemen of the General Assembly, as the Georgia state legislature is called, get bored with fixing budgets, raising taxes, and other official duties, it seems that one of them proposes a resolution to create an official something that's somehow been overlooked.

Sometimes it's pure inspiration. "Georgia On My Mind" became the official state song after Albany-born Ray Charles came to the capitol in 1979 and sang it to a special session.

Official flags have flown over Georgia since January 2, 1788, when it joined the Union as the fourth state. The newest one was adopted in 2003 to replace a controversial flag from 1956 that featured the Confederate States' battle flag. Ironically, the new flag (adopted by popular vote) resembles the Confederacy's national flag, but it's so attractive that nobody seems to mind, and everybody's tired of arguing about it, anyway.

Three alternating stripes of red, white, and red are in the main field. In the blue canton in the upper left corner, 13 white, five-pointed stars representing the 13 original English colonies encircle the gold state seal, which bears the state motto, "Wis-

State Symbols:

Everything's official, even the fossils.

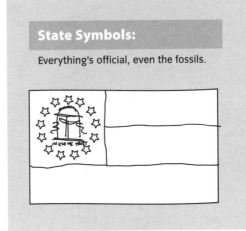

dom, Justice, and Moderation." "In God We Trust" is also printed on the flag.

Other official designations include Pogo, the state 'possum; Georgia peaches, the state fruit; Vidalia sweet onions, the state vegetable; peanuts, the state crop; shark teeth, the state fossil; Vienna's Big Pig Jig, the state pork cookoff; Hawkinsville's Shoot the Bull, the state beef cookoff; and Plains High, the state school (and Jimmy Carter's alma mater).

you know you're in
georgia when . . .
. . . you see Stonehenge

You're driving blissfully down rural northeast Georgia Highway 77 when you seem to be transported magically across the sea to rural Britain. On a hilltop appears to be a scaled-down clone of ancient Stonehenge. What you see is no mirage. But in this case, Elbert County stonemasons, not Druidic priests, fashioned the curious array of six circling granite slabs.

In 1979 a mysterious stranger calling himself Robert Christian commissioned the monument on the edge of a cow pasture, 7.2 miles north of Elberton. He told the president of an Elberton granite finishing plant that what he called "the Georgia Guidestones" would be "for the conservation of the world and to herald a new age of reason." His true identity was known only to the Elberton banker who handled Mr. Christian's deposit. The banker took the secret with him to eternity.

Quarrying, cutting, and etching the stones and putting them in place took nearly a year. Like the 4,000-year-old originals on England's Salisbury Plain, the Guidestones are astronomically aligned. The central stone (16 feet high) is surrounded by four similar upright stones that radiate from the center like wagon wheel spokes. A capstone (9 feet long) is across the top. Slots drilled in the center stone allow visitors to track summer and winter solstices and other celestial events.

On the four upright slabs, "Guides to an Age of Reason" etched in 4,000 4-inch letters—in English, Spanish, Russian, Chinese, Arabic, Hindi, Hebrew, and Swahili—read like New Age 10 Commandments, to wit: Maintain humanity under 500,000,000, in perpetual harmony with nature. Protect people and nations with fair laws and just courts. Avoid petty laws and useless officials.

Those who speak the eight living languages may ponder the John Lennon-ish maxims, but only a scholar of dead languages can translate (or find any typos in) the admonition, "Let these be Guidestones to an Age of Reason." That phrase is etched on the capstone in Egyptian hieroglyphics, Sanskrit, Babylonian cuneiform, and classical Greek.

Stonehenge:

Otherwise known as the Georgia Guidestones: six circling granite slabs in Elbert County with an origin almost as mysterious as England's, even if more recent.

It's 825 feet tall, 6 miles in circumference, and 7.5 billion cubic feet in volume, and it has an exposed area of 583 acres. On a scale it would weigh in at a whopping 6 million tons. Billed as the largest exposed piece of granite on earth, mighty Stone Mountain casts its shadow over a 3,200-acre, multifaceted park and nature preserve that attracts four million visitors annually.

Like an iceberg, the exposed granite (located 16 miles east of Atlanta) is a small part of the much larger mass of granite beneath the surface. Construction crews digging the foundations of large downtown buildings must frequently blast through layers of Stone Mountain granite.

At the crossroads of historic Native American trails, the mountain was a meeting place for Creek and Creek traders. In 1915 it was the re-birthplace of the Ku Klux Klan, which held rituals on the mountaintop until the state purchased it for a park in the 1960s and completed the mountain's most distinctive man-made feature. Begun in the 1920s and finished in 1970, the Confederate Memorial Carving on the sheer north side is the largest high-relief sculpture on earth.

Confederate President Jefferson Davis and Generals Robert E. Lee and Thomas "Stonewall" Jackson stride 160 feet across and 76 feet high. They cover more than three acres, and the deepest point is 12 feet, at Lee's elbow. A 6-foot man could stand upright in Bobby Lee's ear. By comparison, South Dakota's Mount Rushmore presidents are 60 feet tall.

Visitors get a close-up view of the Confederate Memorial Carving as they whisk by in a Swiss-built skylift to the mountaintop. A walking trail goes up the easy-does-it eastern flank. Also around the mountain are a transplanted antebellum plantation, an antique car museum, a sand beach, a petting zoo, a golf course, and a grist mill.

Whitetail deer and other wildlife inhabit the park's woodlands, but the most exotic creatures are microscopic "fairy shrimp" and "clam shrimp" that lie dormant in creases in the rock until heavy rains douse the dome.

Stone Mountain:

Bobby Lee, Stonewall Jackson, and Jeff Davis ride forever on this granite dome.

you know you're in
georgia when...
...you're still stuck on Stuckey's

In the 1940s and 1950s, motorists on America's two-lane "blue highways" looked for billboards directing them to Stuckey's, with its "Clean Restrooms, Pecan Logs." The tidy washrooms were welcome, but what the travelers really craved under a Stuckey's blue roof was a Pecan Log, encrusted with salty nuts on the outside, sweet and chewy with nougat inside.

The Stuckey's story began in the 1930s Depression, when W. S. Stuckey began selling pecans around his hometown of Eastman, in middle Georgia. He set up a roadside stand on U.S. Highway 23, where he sold shelled and unshelled pecans and pecan candy his wife made in the family kitchen. They opened the first Stuckey's Pecan Shoppe in 1937. During World War II Stuckey's sweet treats had such wide renown that they were sold on military PXs and in navy ships' stores.

After the war, when Americans began traveling again, the number of stores boomed. It peaked at more than 100 across the eastern United States by the mid-1960s. In 1964 Stuckey's merged with Pet Foods, and it was downhill after that. America's driving habits were changed dramatically by the interstate highways, which lured motorists off the blue highways and into McDonald's and other big chains.

Stuckey's:

Hey, dad, can we stop for pecan logs? Please, please?

In the 1980s Pet began selling Stuckey's stores for their real estate value. The original Stuckey's on U.S. Highway 23 in Eastman became a Pecan Log-less diner. But never fear, Pecan Log lusters! Stuckey's still lives in freestanding stores and scores of tandems with other food and fuel outlets in 20 states, from Arizona to Pennsylvania, Illinois to Florida. Betcha can't eat just one!

you know you're in
georgia when . . .
. . . you savor *Swamp Gravy*

Small towns dying on the vine often have to use their available resources to get back on their feet. In the early 1990s Colquitt, a town of about 2,000 residents deep in the southwest Georgia cotton and peanut fields, gathered together a sheaf of real-life stories—many humorous, some poignant—and began presenting them in an ongoing theatrical series called *Swamp Gravy*.

One of the vignettes captures the excitement of the circus coming to town. Another recalls a runaway bull that wrecks nearly every "china shop" in town. A housewife remembers the afternoon an alligator "as long as a car" sauntered into her backyard. A father recalls the bittersweet day he saw his only son off to war. Another story is about the simple joys of hanging out on the town square on a Saturday afternoon, waiting for the picture show to start.

The Colquitt-Miller County Arts Council inaugurated *Swamp Gravy* in 1992 with a $700 grant from the Georgia Council for the Arts; the intent was to save the community from the economic decline that has devastated other small rural towns. Plays are presented in spring and fall in a former cotton warehouse that has been turned into a charming theater and museum, with farm implements, antique furniture, and memorabilia donated by local residents. All productions feature volunteer actors and technicians from the local area.

Swamp Gravy:

I believe I'll have another serving.

The organizers initially hoped to attract church and school groups, senior citizens, garden clubs, and others from about a 100-mile radius. More than 15 years later, the plays and other related cultural events attract thousands of patrons from several states.

Few attendees accidentally drop by. Colquitt is about 50 miles from the nearest interstate highway, so patrons usually drive into town with *Swamp Gravy* on their minds. Even when the production is out of season, townsfolk and visitors can relive the stories through colorful murals around the square.

Thanks to *Swamp Gravy,* downtown Colquitt has a historic inn, an Internet cafe, a day spa, and other businesses not typically found in small rural towns.

you know you're in
georgia when...
...sweet tea is your chardonnay

It's a fact: Iced tea was invented in the South. By necessity. One sweltering hot summer day, a desperate soul, his or her tongue dragging the ground, came up with the idea of adding ice to the beverage that Yankees and Englishmen drank hot, with their pinkies protruding daintily from the handles of fragile china cups.

Georgians and fellow Southerners are famous for their sweet tooth—it's believed to be genetic—so, once poured into a glass, the iced tea was laden with prodigious shovelfuls of sugar. It tasted just fine until somebody discovered that the drink was a whole lot tastier if the sugar was added to the boiling water and tea bags.

Now it's proper etiquette to add the sugar while the tea is steeping, then allow the liquid to cool and pour it over ice. A true Southern tea-lover never adds sweetener after the tea has been served. Lemon slices and sprigs of mint add a touch of class.

Sun tea is another Southern specialty. In a washed-out mayonnaise jar filled with fresh water, add tea bags and the desired level of sweetness. Tighten the lid and let the jar sit in the sun for most of the day. When you've finished your chores, a smooth and mellow tea will be your reward.

A hint to sweet-tea novices: If you don't like it sweet enough to set off car alarms, forget etiquette; ask for your Georgia tea unsweetened and add your own sugar.

Sweet Tea:

If it doesn't set off car alarms, it ain't the real stuff.

Born in Ohio, he came to Georgia at age nine, when his family moved to Savannah. He inherited his father's billboard company when he was 24 and turned it in a million-dollar business.

In the 1970s Robert Edward "Ted" Turner launched the Turner Broadcasting System Superstation, which was beamed across the country. The station turned the Atlanta Braves—a team that Turner owned and briefly managed—into "America's Team" at a time when they were so dismal as to barely qualify as "Atlanta's Team."

About his managerial experience, the ever-quotable Turner quipped, "Managing isn't that difficult; you just have to score more runs than the other guys."

In 1980 Turner started CNN, the 24-hour cable news network, from Atlanta. His decision flew in the face of most media experts, who gloomily argued that an all-news, all-day, around-the-world network wasn't possible, especially from a city that wasn't New York or Los Angeles. Turner proved the skeptics wrong when CNN came to the forefront of the news industry with on-the-scene, 24-7 coverage of the 1986 space shuttle *Challenger* disaster in 1986 and the Persian Gulf War in 1991.

In 1977 Turner skippered the winning yacht *Courageous* in the America's Cup Races,

then caused a minor scandal when he showed up for the awards ceremony with a little too much celebration under his yachtsman's cap. He dubbed himself "Captain America."

Turner was married to and divorced from Oscar-winning actress Jane Fonda. He earned his "Mouth of the South" moniker with zingers like this one: "If I only had a little humility, I'd be perfect."

When he retired as a director of Time Warner, Inc., which had purchased CNN in 1996, Turner strengthened his standing as one of America's wealthiest citizens. Much of his wealth has been contributed to worldwide humanitarian causes.

Turner, Ted:

Atlanta and Georgia are proud to have "Captain America" on board.

you know you're in
georgia when...
...Uga is a damn good dawg

In 1892 a billy goat wearing a silly hat, with ribbons tied to his horns, was the mascot for the University of Georgia's first football game. Auburn won the game 10–0, and the goat went back to eating tin cans. A sportswriter way back then came up with the "Bulldogs" nickname, citing the breed's dogged tenacity.

A number of bulldogs served as the team mascot, but the job was open in 1956 when UGA law student Frank W. "Sonny" Seiler and his wife, Cecilia, came to Sanford Stadium in Athens for a home game. They brought a male bullpup clad in a red sweater embossed with a big, black *G* for Georgia. He got the job, and a tradition was born.

Uga I was the first of his dynasty to hear fans woofing and arfing and bellowing "Damn Good Dawg!" His heirs have done him proud. Uga II oversaw a 42–16–3 record during his 1965–72 reign. Uga III (70–13–2; 1972–81) saw Georgia beat Notre Dame in the Sugar Bowl and win the 1980 national championship. Uga IV (73–25–4; 1981–90) escorted Herschel Walker to the Heisman Trophy ceremony in New York in 1982.

Uga V (65–39–1; 1990–99) got his handsome mug on the cover of the April 28, 1997, issue of *Sports Illustrated,* which named him college football's best mascot. He also made highlight reels in 1996 when he tried to take a bite out of Auburn

Uga:

This "Damn Good Dawg!" is the mascot of the University of Georgia football team. It's a job kept strictly in the family.

receiver Robert Baker, who had the temerity to cross the Georgia goal line in front of Uga. And the pooch had a nonbarking role in Clint Eastwood's film version of *Midnight in the Garden of Good and Evil,* based on John Berendt's nonfiction best seller about Savannah's eccentric foibles.

Uga VI, great-great-great-grandson of the patriarch, was handed his responsibilities during a 1999 "Changing of the Collar" ceremony.

When Ugas go to the big kennel in the sky, their remains are interred in a red Georgia granite mausoleum at the west entrance to Sanford Stadium. Sanford is the only American college stadium where mascots are buried where they barked. Guarded by a bronze bulldog, they chase Florida and Georgia Tech receivers eternally in their dreams.

On January 27, 1785, three years before Georgia ratified the Constitution and became the fourth state, the general assembly chartered the nation's first state-supported university. *Chartered* is the key word, since the lawmakers had neither money nor land to actually build a university in Georgia. (The University of North Carolina, which opened in Chapel Hill in 1792, got the honors as the first operating state university.)

In 1801 John Milledge, a member of Congress and future Georgia governor, donated 633 acres on the banks of the Oconee River and threw in some cash for some books and supplies. Only then did the legislature come up with the funding for what is now the University of Georgia. Originally called Franklin College, in honor of Benjamin Franklin, the school graduated its first class in 1804. The original classical curriculum was later broadened to include law, agriculture, and other endeavors.

For his largesse, Milledge got the honor of naming the town that grew up around the school, which took its current name in the early 1800s. With high aspirations for the school, Milledge named the town Athens, after the classical center of Greek learning. The location was considered ideal, as it was "far from the sins of city life and the harmful vapors of the coast."

University of Georgia:

The first chartered state university, and still going strong with more than 35,000 students.

Little did Milledge and the other founding fathers know that the temptations of city life would arrive in Athens at pretty much the same time as the young scholars. Early Athens was a rough little place, with saloons, dance halls, sporting houses, and other bad baggage.

Broad Street, across from the campus, is much more law-abiding these days, but it's still a very lively venue for unwinding students. In the 1970s and 80s, the 40 Watt Club was the showplace for R.E.M., the B-52s and other bands that founded the ongoing "Athens Music Scene."

The academic village that Milledge put on track now has a sprawling modern campus, where over 35,000 students labor in more than two dozen fields.

... nekkid steak, FO, and a bag of rags are gourmet delights

You step up to the counter at Atlanta's Varsity Drive-In, and the counterpersons chorus, like carnival pitchmen, "What'll ya have? What'll ya have?" You reply, "An FO, a nekkid steak, two chili dogs, a bag of rags, rings, and a peach pie walking."

In return a waiter loads a tray with a frosted orange (a creamy frozen orange shake); an undressed hamburger; two grilled hotdogs with onions, mustard, and chili; potato chips; an order of onion rings; and a fried fruit pie, boxed to "walk."

The Varsity is not for squeamish carb- and calorie-counters. Your order comes with enough grease to run a tractor.

Frank Gordy, a dropout from neighboring Georgia Tech, opened the Varsity in 1928. Decades of ravenous Techsters, Atlantans, and out-of-towners have turned Gordy's original snack shop into reputedly the world's largest drive-in eatery.

Still operated by Gordy's family, the mammoth food factory is an essential part of the "real" Atlanta experience—a time-honored rite of passage for dating teens, a fill-up before and after Tech football games, movies, and shopping. It's perfect for proposals and weddings and the best place to go when only a brace of chili dogs can quell your inner hunger.

Everyday, from early morning until after midnight, thousands pull into the vast covered parking area, where car men (not car hops, mind you) rush to take their orders, brought back on a metal tray hooked to the car window.

Inside the art deco building, a conveyor belt carries miles of hot dogs, rivers of chili, and mountains of fried potatoes and onions to the stainless steel counter. There, the goods are passed to walk-ups who fill the 800 school desk seats in five inside dining rooms, each equipped with a TV tuned to soap operas, sports, or sitcoms.

There are five "Junior" Varsitys around Atlanta and another near the University of Georgia in Athens, but regulars swear there's no grease fix like the original at North Avenue and Spring Street.

The Varsity:

Heaven on a hot dog bun.

you know you're in
georgia when...
...you're munching Vidalia Sweets

Just as Idaho is famous for potatoes and Florida for oranges, Vidalia in southeast Georgia's fertile farm belt is known the world over for its sweet-as-an-apple onions. You can eat 'em like a Red Delicious, or try them in everything from sandwiches to soups, salads, and soufflés.

According to legend, the onions were a hybrid developed in the 1930s by Toombs County farmer Mose Coleman. Excited by their pleasant, non-eye-irritating flavor, Coleman sold his onions by the roadside. Pretty soon word got around; cooks craved 'em, and other farmers planted their own fields with the hybrid yellow granex, distinguished by not only its taste but also its shape—round on the bottom and flat on the top stem end.

By the 1970s hundreds of acres were planted, increasing geometrically as demand grew across the United States and overseas. Nowadays, about 275 farmers cultivate Vidalias on more than 10,000 acres. To keep pretenders from bagging hot onions as Vidalias, the Georgia legislature in 1968 defined a 20-county area of southeast Georgia as the official production area. In 1990 the Vidalia was declared the official state vegetable.

Vidalia Sweet Onions:

A Vidalia a day keeps onion-breath away.

What makes Vidalias so mild is a unique combination of sandy, loamy soil and mild climate conditions, including moderate rainfall. On average, temperatures in the growing zone are in the mid-50s in winter and the 70s in spring. Onions mature and are harvested from April through mid-June.

The only thing sweeter than biting into a Vidalia is the $150-million blessing the crop showers on the state economy.

On interstates and busy commercial streets around Atlanta and Savannah, the Waffle House is a friendly yellow beacon, beckoning hungry travelers 24/7.

It all began in 1949 when Joe Rogers Sr. bought a house from his neighbor, real estate agent Tom Forkner, in the Atlanta suburb of Avondale Estates. A regional manager for a now-defunct Memphis diner chain, Rogers got such a great deal on his house that he proposed a partnership for a sit-down restaurant that would operate at a drive-in's velocity.

When they opened their first modest diner in 1955, Rogers and Forkner chose eye-catching egg-yolk yellow for their color scheme. They took the restaurant name from one of the South's favorite breakfast foods.

Their aim was to create a friendly atmosphere in which people could enjoy quality food that wouldn't burn a hole in their billfolds. Through the years the cofounders added a restaurant here, a restaurant there; when Waffle House celebrated its 50th anniversary in 2005, there were more than 1,500 locations in 25 states.

Whether it's in south Georgia, south Florida, west Texas, Colorado, or Pennsylvania, Waffle House maintains a down-home aura anchored by friendly, folksy service and an

all-American menu of waffles, eggs, grits, bacon, sausage, hash browns, burgers, and T-bone steaks. Elvis and Patsy Cline are usually crooning on the jukebox, and most meals cost less than $5.00. (Sorry, but your plastic's no good here.)

Waffles (plain and pecan) top the popularity chart, but the hash browns are so special that they have their own lingo. Regulars order them "scattered" on a grill, "smothered" with onions, "covered" with melted cheese, "chunked" with bits of hickory-smoked ham, "topped" with chili, and "diced" with fresh tomatoes. Avid aficionados order combinations and "all the way."

Waffle House:

Mouth-watering waffles, hash browns, and other breakfast foods at a price you can't beat. Now in 25 states, and worth the drive if yours isn't one of them.

you know you're in
georgia when . . .
. . . summer lasts half the year

In high summer, which theoretically can be on us in mid-May, the sea-level heat and humidity are such that even a quick dash outside will make you feel like you're draped in a wet, woolen blanket. And buzzing, biting gnats and mosquitoes can make even the shortest time outdoors a scratching, itching misery.

It's hot elsewhere in the state, too. The official high of 113 degrees was posted at Greenville, in southwest Georgia's Meriwether County, on May 27, 1978.

But north of the Gnat Line, which crosses the state's midsection, the humidity is usually a few degrees lower and the bugs less aggressive. In the capital city of Atlanta, where the daytime temperature rarely breaches 100 degrees, an altitude of 1,050 feet cools things into the 60s and 70s overnight. And blessed be the Blue Ridge Mountains, where a light blanket is a comfortable overnight companion.

When winter does show its face, never, ever drive on snow or ice. You may be from "up there," where chains and snow tires are standard equipment, but most of us don't have a clue what to do. We don't want to know—that's why we live here.

Stay patient, and keep off the roads. Go outside and make a snowman (if you can scrape enough of the white stuff together).

Slide down the hills on a piece of cardboard or the sled that's been in the garage since you moved here from Buffalo. In a day or two, spring will reassert itself, and in mid-April you can start planning your summer vacation.

If there is a little nip in the air, be assured that it probably won't come close to the state's coldest recorded temperature: −17° F in Rome/Floyd County, on January 27, 1940.

Weather:

Georgia has the best of both summer and winter, in thankful moderation.

you know you're in
georgia when . . .
. . . it's the law, believe it or not

You have to wonder what lawmakers were thinking when they came up with these puzzlers.

Under state law, donkeys may not be kept in bathtubs. Members of the state legislature cannot be ticketed for speeding while the assembly is in session. Official signs must be in English. You have a right to commit simple battery if you're provoked by "fighting words." No one may carry an ice cream cone in his back pocket on Sunday. It's illegal to use profanity in front of a dead body in a funeral home or a coroner's office.

In Acworth all citizens must own a rake. In Atlanta it's unlawful to tie a giraffe to a telephone pole or street lamp, and one man may not ride on another man's back.

In Columbus it's illegal to cut off a chicken's head on Sunday or to carry a chicken down Broadway by its feet on the Sabbath. In Gainesville, the Poultry Capital of the World, you're obliged to eat chicken with your hands; using a fork is verboten. In Quitman chickens may not cross the road, and cars are not permitted to drive on sidewalks.

In Jonesboro you're forbidden to say "Oh, boy."

Weird Laws:

Keep in mind what day it is when you put your ice cream cone in your back pocket.

In Marietta it's illegal to expectorate from a car or bus, but it's perfectly legal to do the same from a truck. In St. Marys spitting on the sidewalk is prohibited after dark.

In Dublin it's illegal to throw rocks at birds. OK, that one makes sense. After all, the southeast Georgia city is a bird sanctuary.

index

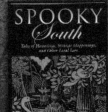

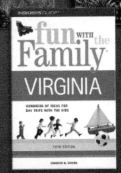
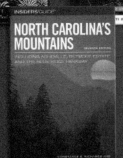